YOUR BETTER SELF

YOUR BETTER SELF

Rabbi Chaim Dalfin

A Guide to
Self-Improvement
Based on Chassidic Teachings

J.E.C. Publications

1ˢᵗ printing, 1994
2ⁿᵈ printing, 1995
3ʳᵈ printing, 1998

Copyright © 1994 by Chaim Dalfin
ISBN 1-56871-086-0

All rights reserved

No part of this publication may be translated, reproduced, stored in a retrieval system or transmitted, in any form or by any means, electronic, mechanical, photocopying, recording or otherwise, without prior permission in writing from both the copyright holder and the publisher.

Published by:
JEC Publishing
1721 45 St.
Brooklyn NY 11204
718/854-4139

Printed in the U. S. A. By:
Moriah Offset Corp.
115 Empire Blvd. Brooklyn, N.Y. 11225, Tel: (718) 693-3800

Dedicated to the eternal life

and spirit of our beloved and revered

teacher, master and father

the sainted

LUBAVITCHER REBBE

REBBE MENACHEM MENDEL

Ben Harav Hagaon v'Harav Hachasid

Reb Levi Yitzchak

SCHNEERSON

11 Nissan 5662 – 1902

3 Tammuz 5754 – 1994

Abraham J. Twerski, M.D.
Gateway Rehabilitation Center
Moffett Run Road
Aliquippa, Pennsylvania 15001

December 15, 1993

Rabbi Chaim Dalfin
821 N. Formosa Avenue #202
Los Angeles, CA 90046
FAX: 213/954-0794

Dear Rabbi Dalfin,

It was a pleasure to review your manuscript. Congratulations on a very fine book.

As you know, I have written quite extensively about the importance of self-esteem and values. I envy you that your audience is one that can appreciate the extremely rich sources for self-esteem and values from the Torah literature and especially chassidic writings. I believe you have succeeded in conveying some difficult concepts in a manner that can be easily understood. These concepts can provide true joy in life even when circumstances are difficult, and certainly the chassidic perspective on a person's purpose in life can give true meaning to one's existence.

I think you have made a significant contribution, and again I congratulate you.

Sincerely,

Abraham J. Twerski, M.D.
Founder/Medical Director

AJT:cv

Contents

Dedication 5
Endorsement Letter 7
Table of contents 9
Acknowledgments 11
Introduction 15

PART I : MIND and HEART   **19**

  1   Mindfulness 21
        Intellect and Passion 27

  2   Expressing Emotions 32

  3   Joy 39
        Letter of the Tzemach Tzedek 44

  4   Our Potential for Change 49

PART II: RELATIONSHIPS   **59**

  5   Loneliness 61

  6   Heart to heart: Sincerity 70

  7   Making Friends: Perseverance 76

  8   Love: Giving and Taking 81

  9   Criticism 89

PART III: SELF and EGO   **95**

  10   The Duality of Ego 97
         Bitul Hayesh 105
         Individuality in Universality 108

11	Selfishness and Self-Esteem	110
	The significance of Chassidic dancing	115
12	Indulgence and Discipline	121

PART IV: A LIVING SPIRITUALITY   **129**

13	Spiritual Perception	131
14	Community: *Farbrengen*	139
15	Patience: *The Nigun*	147
	List of Questions for Self-reflection	153
	Index	155

Acknowledgments

I recall, while I was in rabbinical college, pondering what I wanted to do professionally after I married. The answer came to me as I was studying a chassidic discourse on the topic "Why did G-d create the world?" The answer is that there is no answer, because there aren't any questions regarding the essence of G-d. The only reason G-d gives for His desire to create is "because I want a place to dwell in." Simply put, G-d wants a home, and we make it for Him. Why us? Are we so special and great? Yes; because He said so, we become builders to construct the house.

I realized that my purpose in life was to make a dwelling place for G-d. However, how does one go about this? After more contemplation, it hit me! Whatever and wherever a person is, he needs to express G-dliness to the world. Then that place, person or thing will be in accordance with G-d's will. This is the overall goal of my book.

The individual who most inspired and showed me how to implement this in my daily activities was the Lubavitcher Rebbe, Rabbi Menachem Mendel Schneerson, may he have a speedy recovery and be well. The years, months, days, and hours that the Rebbe shared with my peers and myself via his *farbrengens*, private audiences and writings, gave me the ability to write this book.

I also must thank my *mashpia* — spiritual mentor, Rabbi Yoel Kahan. "Reb Yoel" taught me to bring alive in the real, practical world, the words written in books. He allowed me to spend private time with him, sharing with me the Chassidic attitude towards life. Being a most knowledgeable person in the field of Chassidic philosophy, he showed me how to understand the Rebbe's words.

They were my spiritual parents. My biological parents, Reb Aron Hillel and Miriam Dalfin, raised me in such a manner that I learned that being a Jew, a Chassid, was of greatest importance. They helped me all through my teen years, allowing me to immerse myself in the "ocean" of G-dliness. My mother, may she live and be well, encouraged me to write when I was eight years old. My father taught me, through his experiences as a child in the Holocaust and later as a poor immigrant student in Israel, an intense love for G-d, Torah and Chassidus. Finally, my grandparents of blessed memory, Hinda Fraida and Shlomo Menashe Wiroslaw, were influential in my development as a child. Their lovingkindness and warmth have permeated my entire being.

The *Zohar* says that a man's wife is his other half, and without her he is incomplete. Therefore, my wife isn't family; she is part of myself. My wife, Basya, may she be well, was my guiding light as I wrote this book. Her thoughtful and constructive criticism made this book worthwhile. She made it possible for me to spend many hours at my computer, away from home, while she educated our four precious children. To her I say a very special thank you. My dear children, Menachem Mendel, Shterna Sara, Brocha and Hinda Freida constantly kept me on my feet, alive and awake.

My friend, Rabbi Yanky Winner of Melbourne, Australia, gave me many references and valuable advice regarding the information in this book. Tamar Frankiel, Ph.D., edited the manuscript. Batya Serafini helped proofread and prepare the index. Rabbi's Nissan Mindel, Zalman Posner, Sholom Ber Weinberg and Rabbi Dr. Abraham Twersky reviewed the manuscript. I wish to express my gratitude to Chish Press for recognizing the book's potential and publishing it. My former congregation in Marin County, who throughout my eight years as rabbi and director of the *shul*, *mikvah*, school and Jewish bookstore, gave me hands-on experience in counseling and dealing with people.

Finally, my dear brother Anshel and his business partner Yossi, who is also my good friend, sponsored my writing and work within the Jewish community, making it possible for me to write this book with peace of mind.

I pray that with G-d's help, this book will inspire people to discover their true selves by seeking answers from sources within their own roots. It's all there!

Rabbi Chaim Dalfin
Brooklyn, New York
1998
718/854-4139

Introduction

Much has been written on self-improvement in recent years. But how much of this truly enlightens our lives? Hundreds of books and pamphlets offer only the most superficial approaches, full of the same cliches. Profound and lasting changes in one's life can come only from deeper study of the personality, together with practical guidance to translate knowledge into action. Chassidic teachings, the teachings of Jewish mysticism for the layman, offer a unique approach to self-improvement. They combine study and personal example of the great Chassidic masters with practical steps that anyone can apply. This is effective, not only for adherents of the Chassidic movement, and not even for Jews alone, but for all humankind.

My intent in this book is to give the layman the ability to look into the particular areas of his or her life that needs improvement, and to find a clear, simple solution to the problem, whatever it may be. The primary guide book of Chabad philosophy is the

Tanya. One of its key suggestions is that "the mind is to dominate the heart"; that is, one's thoughts should control one's emotions. In our everyday lives, our emotions are often out of control, leading to disorder in the entire personality. This can be corrected by changing our cognitive distortions of reality.

Generally, the way we think about things governs the way we feel about issues. Therefore, if we change our thinking from negative to positive, automatically our impulses are oriented in a better direction.* For this reason I have called my book *Your Better Self*. This refers to the mind harnessing the emotions in such a manner as to bring out your true and better self. In particular, Judaism emphasizes the study of Torah. Each person has his/her own "part" in Torah, therefore certain areas of study can be especially beneficial. This certainly helps us change our thoughts for the better.

Of course, there is no such thing as a "quick fix." In any area of daily life, when we have a problem, we have to work on it. If we have personal problems or weaknesses, we must work on ourselves. Studying and learning take time; internalizing the lessons takes both time and practice. It is hoped that this book will help students to use their time most effectively by providing sound guides to learning and clear steps to take.

This book focuses on different emotions which are often difficult for us, and on character traits which everyone desires to have. At the end of each chapter, there are suggested readings and sayings, so that the student can delve more deeply into the Torah foundation of the issues that are most troubling. Further, I suggest specific applications and methods the reader can

---

* See Nissan Mindel, *Philosophy of Chabad*, Vol. 2; and David Burns, *Feeling Good: The New Mood Therapy*, pp. 12-13.

implement to improve his or her character. These I call lessons. In this way, anyone who uses this book can combine study, deeper understanding, and practical methods to change his or her life for the better. For this reason I've kept the chapters short and simple. My desire is that this book reach as many people as possible regardless of their background in Jewish thought and philosophy.

I have also included some questions (printed at the end of the book) that you should ask yourself in regard to your character development. For you to see results, I suggest reviewing and contemplating the questions every week. Then write down the answers as you see fit. Finally, locate the chapter in the book that talks about the particular question, and compare the solutions. Doing this over the course of six months will assist you in improving your character. I urge you to do this "homework," and to attend my seminars given once a month in Los Angeles. You may also arrange a private consultation. If need be, I'll come to your community.

May G-d grant that this work bring clarity and truth amongst all people, and ultimately the revelation of our righteous *Moshiach* now!

RABBI CHAIM DALFIN
Los Angeles, California
1994
213/954-1770

PART I:
MIND AND HEART

1
Mindfulness

A fundamental tenet of Chassidus is *moach shalit al halev*,* which means, "The mind dominates the heart." We can express this briefly as the characteristic of "mindfulness." Mindfulness implies that when your heart—which is the seat of your emotions—flares up and goes out of control, you have the natural ability to harness and control those feelings.

G-d has given every person intelligence to be used for specific purposes: for learning, for reasoning, but also for showing and teaching the heart how to be emotional and expressive. To put it in contemporary terms, you feel the way you think.** But this is not something that only an intellectual person can achieve. We know from Chassidic psychology that the mind's domination over

---

* See Rabbi Zalman I. Posner, *Think Jewish* (Nashville, TN: Kesher Press, 1979), pp. 20, 168.

** See Burns, *The New Mood Therapy*, pp. 12-13.

the heart is automatic and inherent* in its nature. The heart actually receives its vitality and life force from the brain; therefore, the heart most naturally follows the dictates of the brain.

When the opposite happens—when the emotions take over—we are acting *un*naturally. That is why it is so disturbing to us and the people around us. We speak of ourselves as being "overwhelmed by grief," "paralyzed by fear," or "overcome by rage." It is as if an alien force has taken over our selves. In fact, no problems can be solved or even tackled, and no growth can occur, when a person's emotions are overriding the mind.

The true meaning of mindfulness is that a person's being is "full" of mind, totally enveloped and controlled by the mind. This does not imply that one should become numb or ignore one's feelings. We can feel our emotions, but within a mindful state where we can assess what is happening. We can see where the feelings are coming from, decide what has priority, and determine whether any of them are signals upon which we should act.

To accomplish this, we can train ourselves to put the mind first, even before our simplest acts. To illustrate: There was once a Chassid named Reb Dovid Tzvi. When he was about to eat, he would always put his hand on his forehead just prior to reciting the appropriate blessing. Then he would make the blessing and then eat or drink. His fellow Chassidim asked him why he had the custom of putting his hand on his forehead. He responded that when he was a child, he had a private audience with the third Lubavitcher Rebbe, the Tzemach Tzedek, who told him: Don't be childish — always remember prior to eating, before Whom you are eating! Afterward he accustomed himself, even as a child,

---

* Tanya, Part 1, Chapter 51; and *Letters of Rabbi Menachem Mendel Schneerson*, Vol. 1, p. 90.

to being mindful of G-d before he actually ate, contemplating G-d and His greatness as the Creator, having created also the particular food he was about to eat.*

The argument is often made that powerful emotions are really out of our control. When an individual comes to discuss personal problems with me as a rabbi and counselor, I often hear, "I can't help myself, that's just the way I feel." This may seem to be the case, but it is not the real situation. The fact is, we have not learned to utilize the true power of the mind, neither in spiritual and psychological matters, nor in very down-to-earth, physical ways.

There was a pious Jew named Reb Moshe Misels from Vilna. He was fluent in four languages—German, Polish, Russian, and French. For this reason, Rabbi Schneur Zalman of Liadi asked him to be a spy for the Russian army. He joined the generals of the French army as a translator. The night before the French were to conquer the city of Vilna, the generals had their maps scattered on the floor and were preparing their attack. Reb Moshe was there to assist them. Suddenly, the door was thrown open. For a moment they thought the Russians had invaded and were going to capture them. However, as they lifted their eyes, they recognized General Napoleon. He stormed in and demanded to know if the final plan was ready for tomorrow's attack on Vilna. Suddenly, he saw Reb Moshe and said to his generals, "Who is this stranger?" Before they could answer, he addressed Reb Moshe directly, proclaiming, "You are a spy from Russia!"

---

* Heard from my spiritual mentor (*mashpia*) at a *farbrengen* (Chassidic get-together) while I was in yeshiva. Printed in *Book of Discourses* of Rabbi Y.Y. Schneerson (1943), p. 143. See there how this is an expression of adult rather than childish actions, indicating the power of mind over emotions.

Napoleon then put his hand on Reb Moshe's chest to see if his heart was beating faster than normal at the fear of having been caught red-handed. Reb Moshe, however, had immediately remembered the Chassidic principle that the mind controls the heart. He responded to Napoleon calmly that he was hired as a translator by the other generals. Napoleon turned away and began speaking to the others. Even on the physical level, Reb Moshe's heartbeat did not give him away.[*]

Reb Moshe, speaking with the famous Chassid Reb Isaac Homlier, said, "The *alef* of Chassidus saved me from death. The *alef* is the first and most important lesson we were taught: to utilize our natural tendencies to serve G-d, specifically the natural trait that the mind dominates the heart."[**]

What we see clearly from this story is one's inherent ability to control the heart and emotions, and not just in an abstract way. The teaching saved Reb Moshe's life because he was able to keep his heart from beating faster under stress. The same holds true for anyone: Whether it is a problem of the heart or of the body, you have the tools to control yourself, and not let your emotions control you.

How is this to be accomplished? The answer is by developing oneself as a deeper human being. Chassidus emphasizes the notion of *pnimius*[***] (meaning inner, deep, concentrated) over *chitzonius* (meaning external, shallow). A person should constantly strive to find his or her inner strength and deeper sources of vitality. Being impressed by facades and flashiness is

---

[*] *Letters of Rabbi Yosef Yitzchak Schneerson,* Vol. 3, p. 312-13
[**] See *HaYom Yom, Adar Sheini* 29, p. 38.
[***] See Jacob Immanuel Schochet, *The Mystical Dimension,* Vol. 3: *Chassidic Dimensions,* p. 198.

the antithesis of what G-d wants of the human being. G-d created the world with perfection, and He wants us, His creatures, to emulate this style by perfecting our characters to the greatest extent possible. When we gain satisfaction from worldly pleasures that excite the body and stimulate our animalistic drives, we are being shallow and external. We are not utilizing our true purpose in life, to be deep and G-dly.

Animals act out of instinct, humans discern with their minds. If we truly reflect on what makes the human being special, we will see that a person's uniqueness has to do with being able to be a *pnimi*, an inward and focused person. For this reason the greatest compliment one could give a Chassid is that he is a *pnimi*: He is developing his fullest potential as a human being.

Depth of personality is attained through two means: mindfulness and patience. The quality of mindfulness gives you the ability to define clearly your strengths and weaknesses and to harness your compulsions. The Mishnah teaches, "Who is strong? He who subdues his evil inclination" (*Avos* 4:1). As Jews, we do not attempt to deny or destroy our desires. Rather, we use our minds to notice, examine and assess our inclinations, in order to refine them in light of our growing consciousness of G-d and spiritual reality.*

Sometimes, however, despite our work in developing depth of understanding, we simply don't have the patience to see the result unfold. This is partly an effect of our culture. We live in the "space age," where everything is immediate: fax machines, microwave ovens, car phones, and the like. We want quick results! The development of a deeper approach to life takes time.

---

* Schochet, *The Mystical Dimension*, Vol. 1: *The Mystical Tradition*, Chapter XV: "In *All* Your Ways..." pp. 72-74

When we feel impatient, we can recognize that this too is a quality given by G-d; we simply have to use our minds to decide when it is appropriate. In other words, sometimes it is good to be impatient. For example, I once received a letter from the Lubavitcher Rebbe, suggesting that I be swift and not procrastinate when I have the opportunity to do good. This advice is an example of applying impatience in the positive way. It is necessary to use the mind to decide whether to be patient and cautious or to act rapidly and with zeal. In situations where it's doubtful whether impatience is harmful or beneficial, a person should be conservative in his approach to life, thinking about things many times before taking action. However, when it comes to things that are clearly good, go for it right away! The Rebbe was advising me to express impatience in a spiritual context: Don't delay when it comes to putting goodness into action.

Nevertheless, in most respects the development of *pnimius* takes time. Mindfulness develops only with practice. To think before we act, and always to think "before Whom we stand," is a life-long discipline.

LESSONS:

> » *1. Remember: You are a human being, so your mind is primary and your emotions secondary. You are not an animal.*
>
> » *2. A human being can transcend his emotions (basic instincts) by exercising his freedom to choose.*
>
> » *3. Practice thinking of G-d in your daily activities.*

> *4. Commit yourself to strengthening your mind through study.*

SAYINGS

> *1. Moach shalit al ha-lev: Mind dominates over the heart.*
> *2. "Reviving the dead": The mind can be cold and dead. A person needs to "revive," to warm up and excite the mind.*

READINGS:

Reading #1

More detailed discussion of the animal drive within the person can be found in the following selection from *Torah Stories*, by R. Jonathan Sacks, p. 202.

INTELLECT AND PASSION

For all this, the purpose of a revelation is that the spirit should change the physical nature of man as well. If man were meant to be pure spirit, he would not have needed a body.* The point of a religious life within the world is to bring every side of human nature into G-d's work: " 'And you shall love the L-rd your G-d with all your heart' — this means, with both your inclinations."**

---

* *Tanya,* Part I, ch. 37
** Devarim 6:5; *Berachos,* 54a

This interplay not only elevates the physical side of man, but also his spiritual life, by adding to it the drive and energy of physical passion. Man as an intellectual being is dispassionate: His emotions and desires are mitigated by the rational control he exercises over them. But animal energy, be it literally in an animal or in the instinctual drives of man, is unchecked and powerful. "There is much increase by the strength of an ox."[*] When the animal in man is no longer at war with his spirit, but is sublimated to it, all its passionate intensity is transferred to a life of holiness.

This is why the Omer was of barley, animal food. Because this was the labor of that period, to transform the "animal soul" of the Israelites, which had remained unaffected by the initial revelation in Egypt.

How is this done? By meditation. Meditation on the nature of G-d awakens love and fear. At first, when one knows that rebellion, pride and animal obstinacy, are still powers within oneself, one must "flee" from them. This is the time of suppression. But once one has left the "Egypt" of temptation, there comes a time of meditation and sublimation, when the two sides of man no longer battle for possession; when the spirit rules, and physical nature transfers its energy.

Reading #2

Study the meanings of *"Pnimi"* and *"chitzon"* in the following selection from *Likutei Dibburim*, vol. 1, chap. 3, section 5, p. 121 and on. (Kehot Publishing)

---

[*] Proverbs 14, 4

"How long shall we stand in a situation that rests on one support?" Within our brotherhood there are a number of chassidim who could be men of quite some stature. That is, they could well be the kinds of people that Chassidus would like them to be. The only trouble is that they satisfy themselves with a level of *avodah* which belongs to the order of the *makkif* [i.e., their spiritual endeavors encompass them as if from a sphere outside themselves, rather than being internalized (i.e., brought to the level of *pnimius*) through the systematic and intellectual regulation of their *avodah*]. They do not have a work plan for their avodah, involving self-cultivation on the level of *pnimius*, and proceeding by graduated stages. Instead, everything is done on the level of *makkif*, as if sporadically.

In bygone days, a person whose *avodah* remained at the level of *makkif* used to be called a *chitzon*. In the eyes of the *temimim* (Lubavitch yeshiva students), the kind of character thus described was despised and out of bounds. There were a number of quite fine students, who toiled earnestly in their [Talmudic] studies, spent their time conscientiously in the study of Chassidus, comprehended their studies (each according to his abilities), and prayed with commendable warmth. But all this was experienced in an outward manner, in a manner of *chiztoniyus*.

Chitzoniyus is related to that which is *makkif*. Whatever is *makkif* is not only outward, or external; this characteristic indeed represents the advantage of that which is *makkif* over its *pnimi* equivalent. For the latter is received within a vessel, which is impossible for a light or power which is *makkif*. But when we say, as above, that *chitzoniyus* is related to that which is *makkif*, this is not meant (so to speak) in a complimentary way. For it is easier to err with regard to something *makkif* than with its *pnimi* counterpart [a person whose *avodah* remained at the level of *makkif*: in the original Yiddish, a *makkifdikin*,] than to its *pnimi* counterpart. A person who is characterized by *chitzoniyus* lives in delusion — he deludes himself; one who is a *pnimi* does not live in delusion. He knows where he stands, and what the particular concept before him means, and is preoccupied with making himself more of a vessel that will be able to absorb the things which occupy him.

A *chitzon*, by contrast, is deluded both as regards himself and as regards whatever concept confronts him. His error can take one of several forms, sometimes veering too much in the direction of ascent, and sometimes too much in the direction of descent. This may be readily observed. There are times when he describes a thing in glowing terms that are well beyond its justifiable proportions, and there are times when he disparages a thing more than is warranted. For a *chitzon* in general is one who exaggerates. It is not that the exaggeration stems from falsehood; it comes from the fact that he is a person who lives in delusion. He fools himself. He grasps concepts superficially, without the inward dimension of *pnimiyus*.

A *chitzon* studies *nigleh*, the revealed levels of the Torah; he studies Chassidus; quite often in the course of his prayers he meditates on the Chassidus he has been studying; and all of this is done with warmth. Indeed there are such whose warmth may be perceived more than that of a *pnimi*. A *pnimi* needs time. He cannot hurry. First he studies; then he meditates on the concept he has been studying; he absorbs it inwardly; until eventually he is warmed by it, and is aroused by it. And this all takes time.

A *chitzon* — with his spiritual situation characterized by the forces of *makkif* — does not need so much time. When he has studied his fill he thinks that he knows his subject. He is so deluded within himself that he truthfully thinks, with the outward truth of his *chitzoniyus*, that he has mastered it. Moreover he is already warm — but his warmth is the outward warmth of *chitzoniyus*.

Whatever a *chitzon* studies, be it in *nigleh* or Chassidus — as soon as he has finished studying, and has not yet even had time to thoroughly digest his subject, he already begins to expound upon it, propounding opinions and arguments, and can even insist on the validity of his own interpretation.

With him, every item of spiritual knowledge and comprehension is inextricably encrusted with coarseness of spirit. To borrow the expression of Likkutei Torah, "his spirituality is coarse." Accordingly, when he proposes a learned argument, he insists on its validity. In the study of Chassidus — which is the *pnimiyus*, the inner dimension of the Torah — his failing, of belonging only to *chitzoniyus* and *makkif*, is even more apparent. When a *chitzon* studies Chassidus it may well be said of him, "Just as he absorbs, so he exudes."

Moreover, a *chitzon* can even be an *oved* (a person who prays for many hours and doesn't indulge in worldly pleasures) — but in this too he is deluded. A *pnimi* knows that *avodah* demands time. It takes a great deal of toil indeed until one transforms a *middah*, a character trait; and even when one has already brought oneself to the point of doing so, one still needs to check oneself critically lest the unwanted trait awaken again. A *chitzon*, however, is not involved with *avodah* on the level of *pnimiyus*, with carrying through a task to its very end, as one should. With him everything remains at the level of *chitzoniyus* and *makkif*. His innate character traits, therefore, remain as they were.

2

Expressing Emotions

If our minds are to dominate our hearts, then we must learn not only how to be aware of our feelings and deepen our perspective, but also how to express our emotions. Modern psychology tells us it is healthy to express the way we feel. But Chassidus explains this on a deeper level.

The little boy Yosef Yitzchak was asleep when his father, the holy Rebbe, Reb Shalom Ber, entered the room with his friend Reb Yaacov Motel Paltova. "What a beautiful shiny forehead your son has!" Reb Yaacov commented. The Rebbe, being the boy's father, naturally reacted with a desire to kiss his little son. As he was about to follow through with the impulse, a thought entered his mind: "Instead of giving him a kiss, I'll substitute a discourse of Torah based on Chassidic teachings." He went into his study and, with the intense emotional energy of the feelings that led him to want to kiss his son, wrote the discourse. In the morning, Yosef Yitzchak woke up. His father told him, "I have a present for you, but I will give it to you on another occasion."

Eight years went by. One day the Rebbe called his son Yosef Yitzchak into his room. "I have a gift for you," he said, "a 'Chassidic kiss.'" He then shared with his son the whole story of what had happened and how he came to write this particular essay.*

Let's analyze this experience. The Rebbe could have easily kissed his son. He would have felt wonderful and certainly would have been honest and sincere in expressing his feelings. However, he realized that to truly show one's love and care for an individual, there is a deeper and more meaningful way of expressing one's emotions. The kiss would be only temporary and the child would not really gain anything from it; he was asleep. The father expressed his passion by elevating it to a more refined expression of love for his son. He gave him something very special and everlasting and shared with him a profound lesson in life.

To express your emotions is indeed healthy. However, you must think of what is best for the other person, not just for yourself. Otherwise you are only helping yourself feel good and not really sharing the positive aspects of the experience with the other person.

What was the gift that the Rebbe gave instead? Words of Torah which are everlasting, and truly the best gift of love that a parent can give a child. Torah is the true expression of love.

Another example: When Rabbi Menachem Mendel Schneerson came with his wife to America in 1941, it was a tremendous event for his family. His wife's father, Rabbi Yosef Yitzchak Schneerson, the Lubavitcher Rebbe at the time, was

---

* Rabbi M.M. Schneerson, *Likutei Sichot*, English translation, Vol. 2, p. 60

undoubtedly overjoyed that they had been able to leave war-torn Europe and arrive safely in the United States. Moreover, his son-in-law was someone with whom Rabbi Yosef Yitzchak could share his purpose and mission in life—Rabbi Menachem Mendel would in fact become the next Lubavitcher Rebbe.

Strangely, however, the father did not greet his daughter and her husband together and immediately upon their arrival. He waited three days before welcoming them. Why? It was the fact that, if he had seen them immediately and both together, they all would have been overwhelmed by emotions. The three days gave all of them time to calm down and put their feelings into perspective. The important thing, after all, was not only the family reunion, wonderful as that might be, but to unite around a common purpose and goal, and that was foremost when they met for the first time in America. This required that their minds be in gear and their emotions be secondary.*

Similarly, in the Torah portion of VaYigash, we see Jacob meeting his son Joseph after not having seen him for twenty-two years. The *midrash* tells us that Joseph kissed his father; Jacob, on the other hand, said the *Shema* and refrained from hugging and kissing his son. What happened, we ask. What about the natural love a parent has for his child? Isn't this cold and inhuman?

However, by looking at this event based on what we explained above, we can understand easily. Jacob could have kissed his son; he could have recited the prayer before or after seeing him. However, he wanted to greet him in a more profound way and give him something more than a kiss, which would be only a transient expression of his own feelings. So he greeted him by

---

* See *Yimei Melech*, a biography of Rabbi Menachem Mendel Schneerson, Vol. 1, p. 545, by Rabbi Mordechai Laufer.

saying the *Shema*.

The *Shema* is the cornerstone of Judaism, the prayer that millions of people had on their lips when they died in the gas chambers. This is the prayer that gives us the ability to give our lives for the Almighty G-d. This was the precious way Jacob wanted to greet his beloved Joseph. He was actually sharing with him the Torah way of expressing emotions. He was saying to Joseph, "Even though you may be momentarily happy, don't be fooled by passing emotions. Your children, the people of Israel, will need something more solid and permanent to be able to counter the pressures of Egyptian culture. Kissing and hugging can only go so far; it is too shallow for the course ahead."

LESSON:

> » *Substitute for your momentary emotions a higher spiritual approach. Be "deep," not shallow.*

SAYINGS:

> » *1. A Chassidic kiss is more powerful than a physical kiss.*
> » *2. Controlling yourself is greater than asserting yourself.*
> » *3. Abstinence makes the heart grow fonder.*

READING:

Learn how Chassidus describes the various levels of pleasure and how our emotional expressions fit into this framework in the following selection from *Kuntres U'Ma'ayan*, Discourse 1, Ch. 2.

[Rabbi Sholom Ber, the Rebbe Rashab (1860-1920), the fifth Lubavitcher Rebbe, wrote the Kuntres U'Ma'ayan in the years following the establishment of the Chabad yeshivah in Lubavitch (founded 1896). In Russia at this time, Jewish life was under attack both from persecution and from the forces of assimilation. Chassidim and their traditional opponents (Misnagdim) had set aside their differences and created an organization, the Society for the Protection of the Faith, to promote the common goal of the preservation of Judaism in Russia. Reb Sholom Ber encouraged this movement and, in his writings, emphasized that the keys to Jewish strength lay in personal devotion in prayer, and in the development of a strong character. The kuntres (literally, "pamphlet") has become a classic text of ethics and philosophy. Its title, U'Ma'ayan, alludes to a quotation from the prophets: "A wellspring shall go forth from the house of G-d and shall water the valley of Shittim" (Joel 4:18). Translated by Rabbi Zalman Posner.]

There are all sorts of pleasures. Enjoyment of delicious food is a gross form of pleasure, as is pleasure in physical things in general, for these are simply animal pleasures. An animal is attracted to whatever it instinctively considers satisfying, ignorant of any other form of good but this, and to this it is drawn. There is a higher form of pleasure, the aesthetic, like that in beautiful music, for this is of a more spiritual nature. Still higher is pleasure from traits of character, for example the favor one performs for another may bring profound satisfaction to a good person. This itself can be divided into categories. The act of kindness might be due to a naturally benevolent disposition without any intellectual discrimination. That is, he performs kindness to everyone regardless of merit, and without any inner purpose. The pleasure in this would be an "animal" pleasure, as it were, an impulse of natural love. It has been explained that the animal is primarily emotive, without any intellect. When man conducts himself and derives pleasure from emotive acts alone, for example these "character traits" we mentioned like acts of kindness, without the guidance of intellect, then he is similar to the animal. All man's emotions and traits must accord with the dictates of intellect.

The trait of kindliness, for example, must discriminate between good and evil. Under [certain] circumstances one must be kindly to the undeserving, but there must be a purpose, a benefit, from this act. Avraham Avinu, for instance, used to provide for pagan wayfarers in the desert, with the intention of proclaiming G-d's presence in the world, and to bring mankind closer to Him. The Talmud (*Sotah* 10a) discusses the verse, "He called there in the name of G-d" (Vayera 21:33). Resh Lakish, through a variation in vowel pointing, renders the reading, "He caused G-d's Name to be called," and as Rashi notes, "There he taught men to call the Name of G-d, the L-rd of the Universe." Resh Lakish goes on to describe Avraham's method of kindliness. "After they had eaten and drunk they would arise to thank him (Avraham). He would say to them, 'Did you then eat of mine? You ate of G-d's. Give praise and thanks to Him who spoke and created the world.' "

This was his ultimate purpose in generosity. It was not mere instinctive kindness, but purposeful, to bring mankind close to G-d through such acts.

The Midrash (Vayera 49) describes how Avraham welcomed his guests. After their meal he asked them to offer Grace. When they asked how, he pronounced with them, "Blessed is the L-rd of the Universe of Whose bounty we have eaten." If the guest consented, he would eat and drink and go on his way. If he refused to thank G-d, Avraham would require payment for the meal, demanding exorbitant sums for wine, meat and bread, calmly explaining, "Who else provides wine in the desert, or meat, or bread?" The guest, realizing his predicament, would thank G-d for His food, and leave.

This is an instance of the trait of kindness, but purposeful, deliberate. All traits must similarly be directed by intellect.

3

Joy

Once we understand something of our emotional lives from a Chassidic point of view, we can begin to discover real joy in our lives. A hint of this comes from a story of a Chassid named Reb Peretz Tzernigov, who was a pious and committed Jew. When he prayed he would cry from one eye and smile from the other. His friends asked him, "How is this possible?" He replied, "The joy comes from meditating on G-d's greatness, and the tears come from contemplating my own deficiencies as a mortal being."[*]

Let's look at this simple story a little more closely. Was Reb Peretz teaching his fellow Jews to be joyful, bitter, or both? At first glance the answer seems to be "both." However, a deeper analysis proves otherwise. Reb Peretz was teaching his friends a

---

[*] See *Tanya*, Chapter 34 (end).

profound lesson in refining a person's character. Happiness doesn't always mean smiling and laughing. If we were able to do that at all times we would be superhuman, or at least abnormal. To be truly happy includes crying from time to time.

How is this so? Reb Peretz saw a weakness in his character, so he cried. But this does not mean he was unhappy. If a person is able to see a negative aspect of his character as an opportunity for growth, this shows that he has a deep inner strength of character, the courage to confront himself. In this light, your weaknesses are no longer drawbacks but, paradoxically, the ultimate expression of how great you are, for they become a springboard in the direction of growth. As it says in the Mishnah, "Who is mighty? The one who conquers his impulses." By accepting the challenge to convert a negative trait into a positive one, you actualize your potential, surmount your obstacles, and build up your sense of accomplishment. This brings true joy.

This is the message Reb Peretz was sharing with his students. When a person recognizes his weaknesses and has regret for his mistakes, he may cry, but this is a true expression of joy and happiness. Reb Peretz was telling his students that even in prayer, one eye must be used to reflecting on one's humanness. A person who appreciates G-d will reflect on himself, and when he is reflective in that way, he is accepting the challenge of the existence G-d has given him. Sometimes this manifests itself outwardly through joy, at other times with apparent bitterness. However, both expressions are coming from the same intention: I am joyful and happy to live life, with the strength You gave me.

In a letter from the previous Lubavitcher Rebbe to a person who was having all kinds of troubles and hardships, the Rebbe encouraged him to be happy. "Be as joyful as you would be if the problem had already dissipated."* He explained further that this is possible only by seeing the resolution of the difficulty prior to its occurrence. He then went on to explain the dynamics of our intellectual understanding that enables us to do this.

There are three faculties of human intelligence: *chochmah, binah,* and *da'as. Chochmah* is the flash of creative thought, a momentary illumination. *Binah* receives and develops the idea, expanding it into a structure of thought. However, it could remain only in the abstract, as pure speculation. The mind must become thoroughly saturated with it, turning the idea into something that is part of us, with conviction. This further intellectual movement is the work of *da'as,* involving attachment and union with the idea. *Da'as* is said to be the gateway to the emotions, for it brings together thought and feeling and brings the issue alive, even though it hasn't yet found expression in any specific emotion of the heart.

In slightly different terms, the three faculties of human intellect can be identified as the three "C's": Concept (*chochma*), Comprehension (*bina*), and Concentration (*Da'as*). As concentration, *da'as* exercises control over consciousness itself, focusing attention where we wish. It is ultimately the chief influence over the form and shape of the emotions. This internalization and concentration play, as Rabbi Nissan Mindel has said, "a decisive and dynamic role in determining the whole personality of the individual."** Your entire personality, at any given moment, is largely determined by the nature, quality, and object of your *da'as* — focus.

Thus, when the Rebbe says, "Be as joyful as you would be if the problem had already dissipated," he is telling us to create a

---

* Letters of Previous Rebbe, Vol. 1, pp. 414, 415, 416
** Mindel, *Philosophy*, 35

solution to the problem and focus on it with intense concentration. This shapes the direction of our emotions and brings us true joy and happiness. The resolution of the issue in the mind, even though practically it is still unfinished, is the key to approaching any problem with a positive, joyous attitude. The Rebbe gives the example of a politician who is extremely happy and confident during his campaign, even though he has no idea whether or not he will be elected or succeed during his term. Yet he feels confident with himself to the extent that he rejoices and throws big parties so that everyone else can be happy.

We see from this letter the importance of being happy prior to that "change of luck" we may be waiting for, before our problems actually disappear. Even while we are frustrated or involved in worrisome things, we must simultaneously be happy. As the Chassidic adage says, "The deepest sorrow and sadness must lead to the greatest joy, and the greatest joy must bring about the deepest sadness and frustration."* The two come together; they don't follow one another, for in fact they complement each other if used properly. This is how it was possible for Reb Peretz to cry from one eye and laugh from the other.

But one may ask even after hearing this story, "How is it possible to actually implement this in our lives? It sounds great and wonderful, but I'm depressed!"

There is an important letter from the Tzemach Tzedek, the third Lubavitcher Rebbe, where he addresses this issue. He gives the following advice:

1. Divert your thoughts from negative things to happy thoughts, even if they are mundane and trivial happy matters in your eyes.

---

* Rabbi Y.Y. Schneerson, *Book of Sichos 5705*, p. 8

2. Study Torah.

3. Pretend and act happy, and you will become truly happy.

4. Don't listen to melancholy music, rather to happy and lively music.

These are steps anyone can take at the very beginning of learning to live in joy.

LESSON:

> » *Practice the four steps indicated by the Tzemach Tzedek to bring more positivity into your life.*

SAYINGS:

> » *1. Who is wealthy? The person who is happy with what he has. (Mishna Avos 4:91)**
>
> » *2. Joy is the vessel for spirituality.*
>
> » *3. Joy shatters all barriers.*

READING:

Meditative reflection on the letter of the Tzemach Tzedek will help you have more joy in your life. Read the selection

---

* In material matters, one who is satisfied with his lot is of the highest quality. In spiritual matters, however, to be satisfied with one's lot is the worst deficiency (*HaYom Yom*, 30 Sivan, p. 66). This is because one must put forth effort continuously to rise spiritually.

recommended below, then spend some time in concentration.

"Part of letter of the Tzemach Tzedek," in Schochet, *The Mystical Dimension*, vol. 3, *Chassidic Dimensions*, pp. 142-47.

Letter of the Tzemach Tzedek

...As for your query about anxiety...one should definitely pray to G-d for cheerfulness, as it is said, "Cause the soul of Your servant to rejoice" (Psalms 86:4), and "Remove from us grief and sighing" (*Amidah*).

Even so, fear or anxiety is sometimes brought on by oneself. In turn, one is also free and able to refrain from it. This is clearly evident from the fact that we are enjoined by a prohibition in the Torah not to be afraid and terrified when conducting warfare, as it is written, "Do not be fainthearted" (Deuteronomy 20:3). Rambam, *Sefer Mitzvos Gadol*, [*Sefer Mitzvos Katan*, and *Chinuch*,] count this as one of the 613 *mitzvos*. Offhand, though, this appears rather strange, for what is a person to do when overcome by fear and dread when perceiving the bloodshed of war? Commandments apply only to situations where man is free to choose to do or not to do, as explained in Rambam's *Shemonah Perakim*, chapter 2.

Note, however, that every soul has three "garments": thought, speech and action.* These are the principal faculties relating to the actions or behavior of man, and through these one can freely choose to think, speak or act as one pleases. It follows then that even if feelings of anxiety do arise, one is able to rid oneself of the thoughts, speech and actions relating to these, especially in terms of not thinking or speaking about them at all,

---

* See *Tanya*, chs. 4 and 6.

and to divert one's thought and speech to the very opposite of anxiety, as explained in *Tanya*, chapter 14.*

In this context we are commanded, "do not be fainthearted"; that is, do not think about fear. Rambam thus rules in the seventh chapter of *Hilchos Melachim* (par. 15): He who allows himself in warfare to entertain thoughts that would alarm him, violates a prohibition of the Torah."

The fact is, that as soon as one stops thinking about it altogether, the feelings of anxiety will disappear of themselves. At the very least, the anxiety will become dormant and will no longer be sensed, and after a few days it will be nullified altogether to the point of no longer arising in his mind — not even as a *machshavah zarah* (alien thought). This indeed is the meaning of "Do not be fainthearted."

Anxiety is nullified by withdrawing our thoughts from it. For all emotions are sustained by the brain-faculty of *da'as* (knowledge). *Da'as* is called the "key compounding the six emotive attributes,"** and is vested in the emotions by means of thought. A removal of the thought, therefore, will of itself remove the faculty of *da'as* from the emotions. This will then prevent that emotion from being aroused, and it simply ceases to be. (This is clearly evident from the halachic ruling stated in *Yevamos* 53b.) The *Gemara* in *Berachos* 60a also indicates that man has control over being afraid or not being afraid.***

---

* See there also ch. 17-19, 25, and 44.

** *Zohar* II:77a; see *Tanya*, ch. 3, and ibid., *Igeres Hakodesh*, sect. XV.

*** That *Gemara* quotes Psalms 112:7 "He shall not be afraid of evil tidings; his heart is steadfast, trusting in G-d," of which Raba said that the first clause explains the second one, and the second one the first one: (a) "He will not fear evil tidings" — because "his heart is steadfast, trusting in G-d" — therefore, "he will not fear evil tidings."

The principal way of achieving a removal of *da'as* and thought from anxiety, is by making sure to divert one's thought to — and vesting it in — cheerful subjects, like the study of Torah which gladdens the heart; setting daily periods for study, ideally together with another person* *(for both nigleh* — such as the Code of *Orach Chayim,* e.g. the laws of the blessings to be recited every morning, the laws of the reading of the Shema, the laws of tefilah, and so forth — and *pnimius haTorah,* a study of *kesavim* (Chassidic discourses) and so forth). A diversion of thought may also be effected by thinking of significant and cheerful subjects of mundane matters.

Moreover, avoid discussing any subjects related to (or possibly causing) dejection, heaven forbid. Always express yourself in a manner indicating joy, as if the heart were filled with happiness, even if you do not really feel that way at the time. By acting in a specific way, one ends up that way.** For man is affected by his deeds and actions to the point that ultimately these will become ingrained in his heart, as stated by Rambam (*Hilchos De'os,* end of chapter 1): "How shall man train himself in these dispositions so that they become ingrained? By frequent repetitions of actions consistent with these dispositions...and thus these dispositions will become a fixed part of his soul."

In summation, then, it is imperative to guard one's thought, speech and action. Do not allow your thoughts to dwell on matters of worry and anxiety, but speak and act as outlined above. If you do so, this will ingrain a cheerful disposition in the soul, and the Almighty will pour forth from above a spirit of joy and gladness of the heart. For thus I heard from my grandfather, the Alter

---

* See *Berachot 63b* and *Ta'anis 7a.*
** Cf. *Shevet Mussar,* ch. 28.

Rebbe, in the village of Piena*: "The Maggid interpreted the verse 'As the appearance of man above upon it' (Ezekiel 1:16): Corresponding to the disposition shown by man below, he is shown from Above!"**

Cf. *Zohar* II: 184b: " 'Serve G-d with joy' — the cheerfulness of man draws upon himself another, the Supernal cheerfulness."

See also ibid., 218a. (My grandfather) therefore prevented me from singing tunes with overtones of sadness in the evening prayer (which I recited prior to his passing, with a melancholy tune), waited for me to conclude my prayer, and then told me the teaching of the Maggid.

Train yourself to prevent any form of melancholy. For man must remove from his heart every form of anxiety, even when there is cause for anxiety...Such feelings are but an enticement of the *yetzer* (evil inclination) and must be cast off like truly alien and evil thoughts. For thus we are commanded, "Do not follow after your heart..." (Numbers 15:39), which is an explicit prohibition (one of the 613 precepts of the Torah) enjoining us to divert the mind from evil thoughts of sin, as stated by Rambam (*Hilchos Avodah Zara* 2:3). In truly like manner one must divert one's thought in our context.***

Insofar as anxiety is sometimes viewed as a virtue, this is only in the proper context of the teaching of our sages not to convey the secrets of the Torah "except to one whose heart is anxious

---

* This is the village where the Alter Rebbe spent his last days and passed away.

** The interpretation reads this verse as follows: "As the appearance of man (below), so it is upon him from Above." See the Maggid's *Likutei Amarim*, sect. 29; *Or Torah*, sect. 134, and ibid., *Hossafos*, par. 19 and 66. Cf. also *Tzava'as Harivash*, sect. 142, and the notes ad loc.

*** See also *Tanya*, beg. of ch. 27.

within him"[*] (i.e., those who are anxious about their souls being afar from the light of the *En Sof*, Blessed Be He), and of this it is said, "This is my comfort in my affliction, that Your word has revived me" (Psalms 119:50).[**]

---

[*] *Chagigah* 13a
[**] See R. Dov Ber of Lubavitch, *Derech Chayim*, ch. 28-29, idem., *Kuntres Hahitpa'alus*, pp. 59-60.

4

Our Potential for Change

As we have seen, a great deal of our psychological make-up, especially our moods and feelings, are based on the way we think about things. We see people and events the way we want to see them, from our personal perspectives. For this reason, each of us has difficulties — for example, in making friends, keeping relationships, and generally being a pleasant person in society. If we were to change our thinking from seeing people in a negative way to seeing them in a positive way, we would increase the number of our friendships and become the kind of people that others enjoy. Likewise for other areas of our lives. As the Chassidic saying goes, *"Tracht gut; vet zein gut"*—which means, loosely translated, if you think positive, it will be positive. Yet this is not so easy. It requires true willingness to change.

To illustrate the point: When the Rebbe, Reb Yosef Yitzchok, was a child, his teacher was dedicated to him not only in regard to his learning, but even more so regarding helping him to develop into a person with appropriate values and ideas. Each night the teacher would come to his room to help him fall asleep, and he would say the following words: "*Morgen darf men ufstein gor andersh*," or, "Tomorrow morning you must wake up entirely different." What he meant was that even though the day had passed, and not all of the child's activities were notable, he had the ability and potential to wake up renewed, not just physically, but also, and primarily, spiritually. His teacher shared this message nightly for many months. In addition, each day he would say, "Even though you said this yesterday and the day before, there is a greater impact if you repeat it every night." Just as G-d renews the creation daily, so each of us can become a new person each day.

The lesson we can learn for our lives is the great importance of continual change. No matter where you think you are now, regardless of whether you think you're doing the "right" thing or not, there is always room for improvement, and therefore you need to grow. As the saying goes, "If you're not climbing up the mountain you're falling down."[*] There is no staying where you are. Yosef's teacher was transmitting the proper attitude toward life, which is that tomorrow you need to be totally transformed!

For change to be successful, we must constantly remind ourselves of three things: (1) who we are, (2) who we can be, and (3) what the ultimate truth is.[**] These three things are of utmost

---

[*] See Rabbi Adin Steinsaltz's wonderful essay in *The Strife of the Spirit* (New Jersey: Jason Aronson, 1988), Ch. 1.

[**] I heard this from my *mashpia* in yeshiva, as instruction given to contemplate

relevance if we are truly interested in changing our characters, and are willing to take some real steps. We must first recognize who we truly are, namely changing beings. We were created out of a change, namely the leap from non-existence to existence. This gives us the ability to be receptive to the idea of change. It enables us to adapt emotionally. We are adaptable, and our creativity means we can determine how we will relate to each change. We have the potential to see ourselves in different ways. We recognize, on the one hand, that what we see today may not be there tomorrow, and what we value may not be important in the larger scheme of things. On the other hand, when we see ourselves as related to G-d, helping to bring G-d's Self-revelation, we take on a new purpose in life.

In 1940 in the midst of World War II, Rabbi Yosef Yitzchak Schneerson had just arrived in America in a miraculous way. One of his first talks was on the festival of Purim, when Torah requires us to be happy. He said, "My heart is depressed for my brothers who still remain in Europe. The bombs are falling and Jewish blood is being spilled in the streets. How can I be happy when they are suffering?" Thus spoke a realist on Purim.

Yet he went on to share a story of a Chassid who, on the morning before Yom Kippur, saw Reb Sholom Ber of Lubavitch in a very serious mood. The Chassid said to the Rebbe, "On Erev Yom Kippur there are two parts to the day. One is the morning, during which the Torah instructs us to eat and drink and be in a happy, festive mood. The second part of the day the Torah wants us to be in a serious frame of mind. So your facial expression of seriousness is inappropriate at this time." The Rebbe agreed, and

---

these three points prior to my going to sleep (as part of the prayers and meditation appropriate at the end of the day).

called for a toast of *l'chaim* in honor of the Chassid.

After repeating this story, the Rebbe said, "A soldier obeys his orders." Here the Rebbe tried to explain the apparent contradiction between his statement that he could not be happy on Purim, and the conduct of Reb Sholom Ber, who *was* able to change his seriousness to happiness. On one level, he could not be happy, because "the mind should control the heart," and his mind was absorbed with the predicament of the Jews in war-torn Europe. But, he taught, there is a higher level, that of the essence of the soul, and that is beyond the control of even the mind, directly connected with the essence of G-d. His essence could rise higher than his mind, being in tune with the desires of G-d—namely, that he be happy on Purim.

Another way of putting this is that a Jew is a soldier in the army of G-d, and when the general gives instructions, the soldiers must follow regardless of their feelings or even their understanding, which might go contrary to what G-d wants. The Rebbe's heart and mind were occupied with the Jews of Europe so he had good reason to be sad; but because he was essentially connected to G-d, the "soldier" in him could say, "it's Purim, and I'm happy inherently because G-d desires me to be happy, and as a Jew I desire what G-d desires. So, on the one hand, my sadness is real; but at a deeper level, happiness is the truth and core of my being. This is where my essence is."

Sometimes we act as if we can't change our feelings or attitudes, let alone our more general personality traits. But the Rebbe teaches us that this is not so. The reason Reb Sholom Ber listened to the constructive criticism from his Chassid was that he was a "soldier" in G-d's camp. Therefore, he was able to change instantaneously. He acknowledged this by saying a *l'chaim*, testimony that the Chassid was right, and that he would change his behavior immediately. But there is also a deeper level to Reb Sholom Ber's immediate turnabout. If a Jew connects to his essence, then he has the ability to conquer his ordinary self completely.* The Torah teaches us that the fundamental criterion for being a Jew is accepting upon ourselves G-d's yoke, regardless of how we feel about it. When as Jews we operate in that mode, we have the ability to change our feelings even under the most severe circumstances.** As soldiers we are conditioned, through our self-control and discipline, to surpass our own natures. Our emotions correspond to whatever is the will of G-d at a particular time, for in our hearts as well as in our minds we are responding to the order of the day, the call of the hour.

The same was the case for the Rebbe, Rabbi Yosef Yitzchak. Yes, Europe was being destroyed and Jewish blood was being spilled. It was very difficult to be in a festive mood. However, the Rebbe was saying, if we are soldiers in G-d's camp, we recognize that now the holiday of Purim is here, and the Commander-in-Chief has ordered us to be joyful; so we answer affirmatively: Yes, Sir! We proceed to carry out the orders sincerely, earnestly, and wholeheartedly, each of us with our entire being.

The previous Rebbe on another occasion said, "A Jew is someone who naturally accepts G-d's yoke, and someone who

---

* See *Tanya*, Chs. 12 and 14, which discuss two different responses to the question of how a Jew has the strength to overcome temptations. In Chapter 12, the Alter Rebbe explains it with the concept of *moach shalit al ha-lev* (the mind ruling over the heart), while in Chapter 14, he uses the concept that by being a "soldier in G-d's camp," it does not enter our minds to separate ourselves from G-d at all; therefore we have the ability not to be in the situation where we are faced with a challenge.

** See Steinsaltz, "A Time for Joy," in *Strife of the Spirit*, Ch. 12.

accepts G-d's yoke is a Jew."[*] That is the simple definition of a Jew. You don't have to be a rabbi or a sage to feel and manifest this identity.

When we want to change, when we want to have a more positive attitude, we can. The only condition is a true desire to change.

When Reb Yosef Yitzchak was four years old, he asked his father why G-d created us with two eyes, while we needed only one nose and one mouth. His father replied by asking him a question: "Do you know the Hebrew alphabet?" He replied that he did. His father asked him the difference between the Hebrew letters *sin* and *shin*. The boy replied that *shin* has a dot on the right side, and *sin* has a dot on the left side. Then the father explained the reason: there are things in life we need to look at with a right eye, and other things we need to look at with a left eye. When it comes to your prayer book and looking at other Jews, always look with your right eye. On the other hand, regarding your toys and candies, you should look at them with your left eye.[**]

From this story we can learn what is important to us as Jews. We need to restructure our values, and the only one who can ultimately make this decision is each of us. As the famous anecdote goes, there was a chicken covered in dirt. Someone came along and tried blowing the dirt off, but there was still some that remained. Suddenly, the chicken gave itself a shake, and all of the dirt came off, even the dirt between its feathers. The moral is: As long as someone else is shaking you, *you haven't changed*. Someone else may have changed, but not the real you. The only

---

[*] Rabbi Y.Y. Schneerson, *Book of Discourses*, 1944, p. 5
[**] *Likutei Dibburim*, Vol. 1, p. 1412

time you really make a change is when you "shake" yourself. As the saying goes, *A kup ken men nit aruf shtellen*: No one can put a head on your shoulders. You are the one who has to decide what is truly important. True transformation is achieved only from within.

The Chassidic self-improvement approach shares with us how it's possible for a person born with a pessimistic view of life to change his outlook to a positive view of the world. It also teaches us how to find the good in every situation, whether it appears at first good or bad. This will mean changing your priorities; and there are things you will have to give up. But the pain is only temporary, and the rewards great. The main thing is that you as a human being have the potential to look at the world and at other people with your right eye, and at the foolish things with your left eye. The only requirement is that you make the choice.

LESSONS:

- » *1. Think positive.*
- » *2. Be open to change.*
- » *3. Choose the right priorities.*

SAYINGS:

- » 1. Tracht gut vet zein gut — *If you think positive it will be positive.*
- » 2. Morgen darf men ufstein gor andersh — *Tomorrow morning you must wake up entirely different.*

> 3. *If there's a will, there's a way. Nothing can stand in the way of will.*
>
> 4. *Ah kup ken men nit aruf shtellen* — *No one can put a head on your shoulders.*
>
> 5. *With your right eye, look at other Jews and into your prayer book; with your left eye, look at candies and toys.*

READINGS:

Reflect on the ideas of being a "soldier" and "accepting the yoke" discussed in the following selections from *HaYom Yom*, 3 Adar Sheni, p. 33 and footnote 1; and Rabbi Menachem M. Schneerson, *Torah Studies*, ed. Sacks, p. 120, sect. 2.

READING # 1. HaYom Yom

The Tzemach Tzedek told a chassid who had mastered the entire Talmud and related works and had a profound grasp of Chassidus: *Kabalas ol** transforms one's being. When a simple

---

* Lit. "accepting the yoke (of Heaven)." Chassidus compares the *avodah* of the scholarly who are intellectually motivated, aware of the depth and nuances of Torah and mitzvos, with the unquestioning obedience of the simple man, motivated by pure faith ("pure" meaning unalloyed by rationales and ulterior motives). Obviously each has a unique quality. Chassidus demands that the learned man acquire the virtue of unlettered, simple faith superimposed on scholarship — bringing him to a fulfillment otherwise denied him. Intellect itself has its limitations, the differing quality of the individual's knowledge, for example. Service based on reason cannot surpass reason, so the *avodah* is always restricted, limited. Furthermore,

servant serves out of *kabalas ol* you can see that he bears the yoke of service even when he sleeps. When a pre-eminent savant and brilliant scholar acquires this sort of *kabalas ol*, even he can attain the height and value of the simple, sincere person who has *mesiras nefesh* — total devotion, self-sacrifice.

READING # 2. The Foundation and the Building of the Sanctuary

The *terumas haadanim* (the offering for the sockets) was obligatory; everyone had to give an equal amount (half-a-shekel); for the foundation of the sanctuary. The *Terumas ha-Mishkan* (provision of materials) was voluntary, of diverse kinds, and was for the structure itself, and its coverings.

If we are to find their analogues in the inner life of the Jew, the *Adanim* must be the original act of *Kabalas Ol* — the gesture of submission to G-d's will, when one forgoes one's independent existence and becomes a vehicle through which the Torah flows. For this act is one in which all men are equal — it does not depend on the particularized capacities of intellect or emotion; it is not the exercise of a power but a state of receptivity. And it is the foundation of all true service, for without it a man is always distant from G-d. If his thoughts and desires form a closed circle, there is no gap through which revelation can enter.

The *Mishkan*, on the other hand, is that which is built on the foundation. It is the articulation of one's faith and its suffusion

---

knowledge is never absolute, so despite commitment and piety there may be gnawing, if unarticulated, doubts. *Kabalas ol* transcends reason and penetrates to, or emanates from, the core of essence of the individual. His involvement is total.

through one's mind and heart. In this each man is different, because intellectual powers and temperament are not evenly distributed, and the extent to which he can grasp in thought, or allow his emotions to be refashioned by, the awareness of G-d which he has achieved through *Kabbalas Ol*, will depend on his particular capacities.

PART II:
RELATIONSHIPS

5

Loneliness

Many people walk around depressed because they are lonely. Spouses lose their loved ones; many relationships are shallow and crumbling, so that many people are single and are lonely. What advice does the Chassidic self-help approach offer for this epidemic?

There is a saying: "Chassidim are never alone."[*] According to this perception, the Rebbe, who is understood in the Chassidic world to be one's spiritual leader, is always with his followers. The model of connectedness and overcoming loneliness thus comes from the relationship between Rebbe and Chassid, spiritual leader and follower.

To understand this, we must get a clearer perception of what a Rebbe really is. A Rebbe, also often called a *tzaddik* or righteous

---

[*] *Likutei Dibburim* Vol. 1, p. 40; *Hayom Yom*, 22 Iyar, p. 140

person, is a person who can teach his followers how to serve G-d because he himself, by his example, shows that he is always and completely devoted to the service of G-d. Many sources tell us that in each generation there is at least one such person, sometimes several, who have achieved a level of spiritual awareness where they follow G-d's will completely and have no self-interest. This is why Chassidim can feel so close to their Rebbe: Since the Rebbe operates without egotistical interest, he can help his followers in a way that no ordinary person can. The Rebbe can become, in an extraordinary way, an always-open channel, a continuously flowing stream, between his followers and G-d. "Though continents and oceans may separate him from his Rebbe," writes Rabbi Zalman Posner, "he never feels that he has been cut adrift. As the late Rebbe once put it, 'Oceans do not separate us; they connect us.'"*

The openness between Chassid and Rebbe is always present on the spiritual level. Ideally, it could be that way among all Jews. Practically speaking, however, it is not. And practically speaking, Chassidim may feel loneliness sometimes. What if they live far away from their Rebbe? What about the feeling of isolation when the Rebbe passes on? How can they be certain of a continuing connection?

In a letter from Rabbi Yosef Yitzchak Schneerson to a Chassid who was yearning to see and hear the Rebbe, Rabbi Schneerson explains that something special was accomplished by the revelation of Chabad Chassidus. Prior to Chassidus, Torah was studied, but the service of prayer was not a focus in the Jewish world, and material needs could not be met due to the difficult times. Moreover, the teachers and scholars of Torah were in a

---

* Posner, *Think Jewish*, p. 29

totally separate world from their students. There was a feeling of isolation among the disciples and among the teachers because the two groups were not united; particularly, the two were separated in regard to day-to-day issues. Chassidus revealed the G-dly capability that each and every one of us has, not to feel alone. This feeling was also shared by the Rebbe, in that he doesn't feel isolated from his followers.[*]

To understand this in turn, we must explain the true nature of a Jew. In the *Tanya*,[**] the Alter Rebbe shares with us the concept that the true life of a *tzaddik* is the spiritual, not the physical. Prior to his passing on, the *tzaddik* is bound by the physical limitations of the body; after his passing, he is no longer limited and can relate to us with his true essence, the spiritual, which is limitless. But this is true also of every Jew. Since every Jew possesses a Divine soul which is limitless,[***] we have the potential to live in the same manner as the *tzaddik* whose entire life was an expression of the Divine soul. Still, we may feel that a person such as a *tzaddik* is on another level of existence entirely, that we can never be close to such an individual. Yet, Chassidus teaches, it is not only possible, but actually happens. We can understand this by comparison of the soul and the body: The way that G-d unites the soul and the body is miraculous.[****] Rationally, they are two diametrically opposed forces, the spiritual and the physical, which cannot unite; however, G-d brings them together by a miracle into complete union. Moreover, both the soul and the body feel one another in the

---

[*] *Letters of Rabbi Yosef Yitzchak Schneerson*, Vol. 13, p. 273
[**] *Tanya*, section 4, letter 27
[***] *Tanya*, Section 1, Chapter 2
[****] Morning Blessing, "*Elokai Neshamah*," *Siddur Tehillas Hashem*, Kehot, pp. 6-7

most intimate way. The body feels it can't live without the soul, and the soul feels it must have the body to be complete. This is true unity: Neither functions fully without the other. Therefore, a healthy soul needs a healthy body, and a healthy body must have a healthy soul.

By analogy, we can understand what happened with the innovation of Chassidus. Prior to Chassidus there were teachers and students, both of whom indeed learned Torah at a very high level. However, they were in two worlds: the student limited by the physical realm, and the teacher living on an intensely spiritual level. With Chassidus came the possibility of a new level of relationship with a unique combination of the so-called two worlds, "body" and "soul." This unity permeated the inner depths of both the Chassid and the Rebbe, the result being that even when Rebbe and Chassid are physically far apart, in two different places on earth, neither is lonely. This is possible because Chassidus focuses on helping each of us connect with the true self, the *neshamah* or soul, so that we truly manifest this G-dly gift of transcending the physical.

What needs to be clarified is precisely how to do this: not only to know in our minds that we are not alone, but also to create the awareness of togetherness at all times and places.

First, on the mundane level, we can enrich our connections with the Jewish people. In a letter from the current Lubavitcher Rebbe, Rabbi Menachem Mendel Schneerson, he instructs a woman who was suffering from depression and loneliness to get involved with groups of people and socialize with them. The Rebbe points out that it is human nature to be social, each person to a different degree. Just as, if you're standing on the edge of a pool and are contemplating swimming, but you don't know how to swim; if you remain on the outside of the pool, you'll never learn how to swim. The only way you learn is by jumping in. So it is with removing loneliness and depression: One must begin by "jumping in" to a social setting. Then one will eventually benefit from that first forceful step.* However, we are not speaking of socializing just as an excuse to party. The Rebbe meant that being with people helps to change one's mood.

A further point is to join to circles of other Jews, to find ways to become connected to the Jewish people. All Jews are brothers and sisters and, like family, their very presence lends security and helps create a strong foundation on which to build a life, together with the recognition that we are not alone in the world. In another letter, the Rebbe quotes a very famous Chassidic saying, in the name of the great Chassidic masters: "It is worse to be alone in heaven than with other [Jews] in hell!"**

We can develop a sense of connectedness on a deeper level. The fifth Lubavitcher Rebbe, Reb Sholom Ber, said just before his passing, "I'm going to heaven, and I'm leaving my writings with you." At first glance it seems that these are two separate thoughts: his passing on, and his leaving his writings to his Chassidim. In truth, however, he was saying something more profound: The way his followers will be able to unite with him after his passing is through studying the writings which he left for us. If you connect with his teachings, you will grasp him not merely in a physical sense but in the greatest possible way, in an eternal bond.

How is this so? Obviously, the writings of the Rebbe would remind his followers of him. But this would not necessarily cure

---

* *Letters of Rabbi Menachem Mendel Schneerson*, Vol. 18, p. 534, Letter 7008
** Ibid., Letter 1774

loneliness; indeed, the memories could in some cases make his followers miss him more. The writings and teachings that the Rebbe stood for were teachings of Torah, particularly of Chassidus. Chassidus is the section of Torah that teaches the inner aspects of Judaism, focusing on how we can transform ourselves into G-dly beings. The founders of Chassidus, the Baal Shem Tov and his disciple the Maggid of Mezritch, taught in ways that transcend the rational mind; the Rebbes who followed brought their teachings into the realm of intellect so that we can all learn them.* The Rebbes taught from their own spiritual knowledge, from an awareness of being close to the presence of G-d. By studying the concepts they taught, individuals can become irradiated with these ideas to the extent that joy and vigor enter their lives, and they experience a feeling of togetherness with G-d.** This is the ultimate reason why the Rebbe's writings would help his followers overcome loneliness: They would come nearer to the Rebbe's own essence and to G-d, where it would be impossible to feel alone.

The primary reason why many people feel lonely is that they don't have anything eternal in their lives. If a relationship is based only on material and physical gratification, then of course you will feel lonely when that is not provided. When you are single and don't have your "other half" to enjoy life with, that can make you very sad. What we need to find in our lives is meaningful, everlasting relationships which go beyond the physical and psychological. For a Jew, the Torah is permanent. It brings a

---

* See *The Essence of Chassidus*, Kehot, Ch. VI, note 44.

** Central concepts of Chassidus include the creation *ex nihilo*, the constant renewal of creation, the ultimate purpose of mankind, and the importance of serving God with joy.

person to a state of connection with something that lasts even after death, indeed forever. It is said that every person has his or her own personal "share" in Torah, meaning that each person's essence is connected to a particular part of Torah; especially so in the case where one has written Torah literature. These writings were of course his "share" in Torah. Therefore, when we learn the parts of Torah that were written by another person, we can connect with what that person is, or was, really about. Then there is no reason to be sad, because the essence of the person is always with you. Even when the person has not written anything, if we emulate his ways and go on living as he would wish, continuing to support what he would support, we thereby cause him to be with us. His "life" continues, for the legacy gives life.

Whether you are missing a certain relationship or you are single, widowed, or divorced, in the end—though this is not easy and may even be painful—the important thing is to become spiritually oriented. Recognize that the material aspects of a person are only temporary. In the Torah, the essence of everyone you are missing can be found. You will come to feel that you aren't alone because the writings of the Rebbe are here with you.*

LESSONS:

» 1. *Remember: All of the Jewish nation is your family. Get involved in organizational activities where there are others around, even if you feel anti-social!*

» 2. *Make it your conscious intention to connect*

---

* See *Tanya*, Section 4, *Iggeres HaKodesh* 27, p. 292.

with spirituality, which is permanent.

» 3. If you are missing a certain person, study Torah, particularly those areas of Torah that bring to life the person you are missing, for example, sections that he or she liked to talk about.

SAYINGS:

» 1. Chassidim are never alone.
» 2. It is worse to be alone in heaven than with others [Jews] in hell!

READING:

Spirituality is the true and eternal life of a Jew. *Tanya*, section 4, ch. 27 provides an elucidation of the above.

It is stated in the sacred *Zohar* that when the *tzaddik* departs he is to be found in all worlds more than in his lifetime...Now this needs to be understood. For, granted he is to be found increasingly in the upper worlds, because he ascends to there; but how can he be found more in this world?

This may be explained along the lines of what I received on the saying of our sages, of blessed memory, that "He has left life unto all the living."

As is known, the life of the *tzaddik* is not a physical life, but a spiritual life, consisting of faith, awe, and love. Thus of faith it is written: "And the *tzaddik* lives by his faith." Of awe it is written, "The awe of the Lord is for life." And of love it is written: "He who pursues *tzedakah* and *chessed* will find life," and *chessed* refers to love.

These three attributes are prevalent in every world to the topmost of levels, all proportionate to the levels of the worlds — one higher than the other by way of cause and effect, as is known. Now, while the *tzaddik* was alive on earth, these three attributes were contained in their vessel and garment on the plane of physical space. This is the aspect of the *nefesh* bound to his body. All his disciples receive but a radiation from these attributes, and a ray [from them] radiating from beyond this vessel by means of his holy utterances and thoughts. That is why our sages, of blessed memory, said that a person cannot comprehend his master... But after his passing, as the *nefesh* [which remains in the grave] is separated from the *ruach* [i.e., these three attributes] which is in the Garden of Eden, whoever is nigh unto him can receive his part from the aspect of his *ruach* because it is no [longer] within a vessel, nor on the plane of the physical space. Thus is known the saying of our sages, of blessed memory, with reference to our father Jacob, peace be to him, that "The Garden of Eden entered with him." Likewise it is stated in the book *Assarah Maamaros* that the sphere of the Garden of Eden spreads itself around every person, and in this sphere are recorded all his good thoughts and utterings of Torah and Divine worship (and likewise to the contrary, Heaven forbid; they are recorded in the sphere of the Gehenna, which spreads itself around every person). Thus it is very easy for his disciples to receive their part of the essential aspects of their master's *ruach*, i.e., his faith, his awe and his love wherewith he served the Lord, and not merely a ray thereof which radiates beyond the vessel. For the essential aspect of his *ruach* is raised, elevation upon elevation, to become absorbed in his *neshamah* which is in the upper Garden of Eden, in the supreme worlds.

6

Heart to Heart: Sincerity

"Words coming from your heart will penetrate the other person's heart." Such were the words of our Talmudic masters, but we have lost touch with this fundamental aphorism. We live in an age in which everything is plastic and steel, from credit cards to automobiles. Relationships have taken on some of that crassness and superficiality. We need to reexamine our values.

Truthfulness and sincerity have, in the past, always been the linchpins of society: the more open and honest you were, the better liked you were. Today, a person who is not politically "savvy" is a failure. We avoid "saying it the way it is," and we think people will like us more if we beat around the bush. This is a great mistake. It is, in fact, the source of the total breakdown of relationships.

There were once two young girls who were very intelligent. Their father hired a teacher, who decided to teach them only those parts of Judaism that made logical sense. He refrained from telling them stories dealing with matters which are beyond the human intellect. Particularly, any story that told of a miraculous occurrence was eliminated. He felt that such stories were symbolic of metaphysical notions, which the girls were too immature intellectually to handle. If he simply told them such stories and expected them to accept them on faith, he felt he would alarm them and perhaps scare them away from Judaism.

When the grandfather of the girls heard about this approach, he immediately fired the teacher. Why? The fundamental basis of being a Jew is pure, sincere belief. Everything else follows from there. The teacher was teaching human philosophy, the latest in rationalism, but not Judaism. Moreover, this true-life experience is not relevant only to Jews; it contains a lesson essential for every human being to learn.

Simplicity is a trait that emulates the Oneness of G-d. If G-d were to have color, shape, and definition, He wouldn't be G-d. As soon as we describe Him, we are limiting Him to the boundaries of that description. The only true "description" of G-d is that He is simple, in the sense of being beyond description. G-d totally transcends boundary, form, or composition. Simplicity, in relation to G-d, can be understood as "unformed abstractness," or his true infinity. For this reason, our traditional stories are often simple, and Chassidic teachings admire the "simpleton." He is the quintessential manifestation of G-d in human form, for he cuts through the layers of superficial covering to the truth.

In relationships, simplicity brings forth truth and therefore friendship. How many people can say they have one true friend who would do anything on earth for them, who would give them his bread before taking for himself? People constantly tell me they have no true friends. The reason is because we aren't simple and direct, sincere and truthful. Everyone can see that we are acting most of the time, as if we were on stage, performing in masks for the public. No one is fooled; people are intelligent and can see through the disguise.

Simplicity doesn't mean the lack of cleverness; it's not synonymous with foolishness. The one despised human character is the "fool," who denies reality, exaggerates, or fails to see the truth; whereas simplicity is the truth itself. To become ordained, a rabbi must know the four parts of the *Code of Jewish Law*. But there is a saying that there's a fifth part that is not in writing: having common sense. If a rabbi is a genius in Torah study but lacks common sense, he's not a rabbi you want to consult. The fifth part of the law means simple practicality, a keen sense of being able to apply the law to the realities of day-to-day life, offered with sincerity.

Simplicity and sincerity are important with respect to ourselves as well. When it comes to self-improvement, we must be open and honest with ourselves to properly assess our strengths and weaknesses. Some of us don't allow ourselves to discover our shortcomings. We fear that if we were to look inside of ourselves, we would discover areas that are very painful. So we let these issues stay "asleep," and we rationalize, saying we will deal with these later. We all know the result: a character shattered by pain, covered up with a false smile.

The Chassidic self-help approach teaches us how to allow ourselves the liberty of looking inside, yet not becoming depressed by it. That way is through sincerity and simplicity. G-d has created every human being with positives and negatives; we are not like G-d, Who is only strong. He gives us weaknesses precisely so that when we choose wrongly, revealing our weaknesses, we will discover that it's all right to make mistakes. All He wants from us is truthfulness. A mother tells her child, "It's okay to fall down, that's the way you learn to walk." Chassidism shows us the drives within every human being: the human, or rational, and the animalistic. We were created this way so that we can have the opportunity to choose right or wrong. If we had only good and rational thoughts, with no desire to go astray, we would be angels, not humans.

Indeed, what G-d wants from us is truthfulness. Truthfulness here means a sincere account of oneself, based on self-examination. This is the significance of the aphorism, "Know yourself." We can serve G-d properly only when we are fully aware of our own inner selves, including all our deficiencies and our good qualities.*

When we recognize this, we can allow ourselves to look within. The main thing is commitment to truthfulness and simplicity. For this very reason the founder of Chassidism, the Baal Shem Tov, showed extraordinary love for the common folk, who were peasants and ignoramuses from the point of view of Jewish scholarship. But his philosophy wasn't just for them. It was a true expression of what a person is really about: simplicity. In a certain sense, the simple people were the manifestation of G-dliness in human form. By giving extra attention to the simple, ignorant Jews, he also taught this lesson to the Talmudic scholars of his day.

---

* See *HaYom Yom*, 26 Cheshvan, p. 107; 25 Nissan, p. 48; and 27 Adar I, p. 32.

LESSONS:

> 1. *Be simple, not sophisticated.*
> 2. *Allow yourself the privilege of looking within yourself.*
> 3. *Understand that G-d has created you with strengths and weaknesses.*

SAYINGS:

> 1. *Words from your heart enter the other person's heart.*
> 2. *Simplicity and G-d are one.*

READINGS:

Earnestness is the highest form of self-examination, as we see in the following selection based on *HaYom Yom*, 4 Tishrei, p. 93; and 24 Iyar, p. 56, final paragraph:

Reading # 1.

A resume of my father's explanation (of the first method of *teshuva*):

Tamim..., "Be sincere with G-d."[*] This represents the *avoda* of *teshuva* that comes through sincerity. Sincerity, or "wholeness," takes any number of forms and has many levels. In reference to

---

[*] Devarim 18:13.

teshuva the highest form is wholeness of heart — called "earnestness"; as the Torah says of Avraham, "You found his heart faithful* before You."

Reading #2

With the advent of Mashiach, there will be revealed the superior quality of the traits of simplicity and wholeheartedness found in the *avodah* of simple folk who *daven* and recite Tehillim with simple sincerity.

---

* I.e. "whole"

7

Making Friends: Perseverance

Every few years our modern culture gets bored with being contemporary and looks for outdated styles and the fashions of former years. We see this most commonly in clothing: What was out yesterday is in today; the latest styles are more and more traditional. We should look at Judaism all the more: Our heritage is rich with age-old "styles" that are very contemporary and modern if applied in the proper way.

Having friends is one of these so-called "old-time" fantasies. In my counseling, I have heard people say over and over again that they don't have friends, that everything and everyone is cold and shallow. This is a function of the "me generation," with its selfishness and egocentricity. A person once confided to a friend of mine: "I come first, second, and third." It's time to get back to traditional values that will enrich our lives, and one of these values is making and having friends.

The Torah's handbook on moral and ethical values is *Ethics of the Fathers*. A saying mentioned there tells us directly: "Acquire for yourself a friend." Part of living a moral life is to have a friend. However, a deeper look at the exact wording shows us something even more important. You should have a friend; but what if you have tried and tried, and you don't have a friend? What should you do? "Acquire" a friend—go and purchase one.

A person should go to the extreme of "buying" a friend. This doesn't necessarily mean to pay money to someone to be your friend (although this is what people seem to do with their therapists). What it really says is that a person has to do everything within his power to have a friend. What does "everything in your power" mean? Imagine an art collector who has at last found the missing Picasso he has always wanted: He will go to any length to get it, expending his entire fortune, traveling around the world, taking time off from everything else to negotiate the deal he wants. He is so determined to have that item, he'll "go to the ends of the earth" to get it. The same is true regarding a friend. Our pursuit of friendship should be with complete determination, as though it were the dream of our lifetime, almost within our reach.

The quality that is necessary for this pursuit to be successful is known as perseverance. To get what you want, you must be properly focused. You must have goals and constantly be attending to how they are being fulfilled. There is a story of a person who came to work every day, but the work was slow and money wasn't coming in. A friend advised him to study Torah during his lunch break. Suddenly, during lunch hour he became extremely busy with business. He mentioned this to his friend with some amusement. His friend said, "What you were missing was being focused on the goals you had, namely to make a livelihood. When I suggested studying Torah during your break, I knew the forces of evil wouldn't allow you to continue studying Torah, so they would distract you by sending you more clients!" We learn from this anecdote the importance of being focused on our *ultimate* goals. It takes tremendous perseverance to accomplish them.

Chassidus explains this idea with the concept of *ratzon*, willpower. The reason willpower is so strong and powerful is that it is close to the essence of the soul. Most other forms and expressions of the soul are only manifestations, mere glimpses of the soul's true being. The willpower, on the other hand, is essential (see Reading).

There is a saying among Chassidim: when the Rebbe is not available for advice, and you have a dilemma, what should you do? Go to a friend and listen to what he tells you. What if you are in a place where you have no friend? Go to your enemy and do the opposite of what he tells you. What's the logic? Your friend wants the best for you; your enemy wants the worst. But even more, this saying suggests the importance of a friend; he is equivalent to the Rebbe in certain circumstances.

How do we know if we have a true friend? Chassidus teaches that a true friend feels the other person's joys and misfortunes regardless of where he is. If your friend is in Australia and you're in America, you will feel happy when her daughter is getting married. Is this ESP? No, it is simply that true friendship is boundless and timeless; its impact reaches across the oceans, to the extent of motivating you to pick up the phone or write a letter, wishing your friend well. Affection knows no barriers and transcends the limits of time and place.*

King Solomon says in the book of Proverbs, "A concern in

---

* *HaYom Yom*, 26 Shevat, p. 23

a man's heart, *yasichena.*" Our sages in the Talmud offer two explanations of the last word: "remove it," meaning remove the concern from the mind, or "discuss it with others." The third Rebbe of Lubavitch explained, "with others," who are others only in the bodily sense, but really are completely united with him, for they empathize with him.* A friend is one who feels for you, an ally, one whose interests are your interests. King Solomon was addressing anxieties and worries; his advice is to open ourselves up to others who are more like an extension of ourselves, namely our friends. The advantage they have is the ability to see us more objectively, to identify faults that we don't see. So to rid yourself of tension and anxiety, get yourself a true friend. You can do that only by making friendship a true priority in your life.

LESSONS:

» *1. Do whatever it takes to have a friend, including "buying" one.*

» *2. You make your own choices and decisions—don't blame anyone else.*

» *3. Sharing your anxieties with your friend helps them to dissipate.*

SAYINGS:

» *1. Acquire for yourself a friend.*

» *2. All Jews are friends.*

---

* *HaYom Yom*, 25 Sivan, p. 65

READING:

From *Chassidic Dimensions*, Rabbi J.I. Schochet, vol. 3, pp. 213-14

In a paraphrase of the maxim that "everything depends on the will,"* the Rebbe states:

It is not we who count — we with our weaknesses and limited capacities. It is our will to do a task that we realize is important. Success is not in our hands, it is G-d's. But we have to will to do what He demands of us, and in that will all our weaknesses and insufficiencies wane and become insignificant.**

---

* *Zohar* II:162b. Cf. *Megilah* 6b; Maimonides, *Hilchos Teshuvah* 5:1

** Kranzler. This statement may be taken as a succinct synopsis of the Rebbe's approach and attitude, reflecting his ever-recurring theme that "*hama'aseh hu ha'ikkar*" — action, actually doing, is the essential thing! (*Avos* 1:17; see *Zohar* 1:99b)

8

Love: Giving and Taking

So much of our modern culture centers around love, its power and its weakness. The result, however, seems to be a near-total disaster. The divorce rate is higher than ever, and what seems to be "true love" ends up being shallow and divisive. It is not necessary for us to get depressed, however. What we need is an alternative approach to love and its great potential.

For hundreds of years, philosophers have defined the human being as a social being. This was observed by Maimonides, the great Jewish philosopher of the early thirteenth century. He explained that G-d created humans in order that we may transform our surroundings by transforming ourselves, the people around us, and the environment. Otherwise, why would G-d have sent us to this earth where there is so much confusion, chaos, and concealment of G-dliness? The reason is that G-d wanted us to interact with other people and things.[*] He already had celestial beings who were totally self-sufficient. Not social beings, they function on their own. G-d created us for a different purpose, putting us here on the physical earth.[**] The conclusion: We need other people in order to function; otherwise we deteriorate.

It is of course true that we must have love for ourselves. But we must recognize that when a person loves himself there can be two paths, depending on the extent of the self-love. If you over-indulge and become obsessed with yourself, this will lead to the opposite of love toward others. It will be as if no one else exists, for you always think of yourself as number one.

There was a Chassid who came to Rabbi Menachem Mendel of Lubavitch seeking his guidance. His problem, he said, was that people in his synagogue were "stepping all over him" and not giving him the respect he felt he deserved. When he asked what he should do, the Rebbe replied, "Who asked you to spread yourself all over the shul, so that whenever anyone takes a step it's on you?"[***] The implication is that the man was the cause of his own misery: It was his own sense of self-importance that made him believe he wasn't getting enough respect. We tend to expect everyone else to see things the way we do, and if they don't we feel we aren't getting our due.

The second approach to loving yourself is more balance. You feel that the other person is as great or greater than you, and they feel that respect and admiration. They are aware you have

---

[*] See Rabbi Y.Y. Schneerson, *Letters*, Vol. 1, pp. 150-51, letter 147.
[**] See the Talmud, tractate *Shabbos*, p 88b-89a, where there is a discussion of the giving of the Torah to human beings versus to the angels.
[***] *HaYom Yom*, 10 Teves, p. 10

made them a priority in your life; the result is that they reciprocate with a feeling of love toward you. True, you love yourself: This is a fact, a state of being, an essential self-love which exists in every healthy human being. However, you realize that every person is one piece in the vast puzzle of creation. In this puzzle no one can fit in or find his "place" without everyone else finding his place. Only when all of us fit together will the picture be complete. This is accomplished by thinking of the other person first and yourself second.

Thus, seeking love and approval is very natural, as with the Chassid of Rabbi Menachem Mendel. However, the Torah instructs us as to how to express this love and when it is appropriate: We must see ourselves and others in the context of our greater purpose on earth. This means we must take a spiritual approach to love.

There was once a great Rabbi called the Apter Rebbe. He once called his son and asked him to touch his hand. The son did. The father then asked him, "What do you feel?" The son replied, "I feel a physical hand." The Rebbe responded, "Because you touch me with the physical, therefore you feel the physical. If you had "felt" me with your soul you would have felt my soul!" What was the rebbe teaching his son? The way you are is the way you perceive others. If you approach things from a physical perspective, that is what you will experience; on the other hand, if you approach things spiritually, you will be able to sense another person's spirituality.

This is essential to understanding the Torah approach to love. We must learn to perceive others from the highest possible point of view. If you are materialistic and oriented toward the physical, you will think of everyone else that way. If you are selfish you will see everyone else as selfish, and you won't have loving and caring relationships with friends. If, however, you look toward the spiritual, "feeling with your soul," you will be able to see the unique goodness of the other person. In practical terms this means you will put the other person first and yourself second. Then, because you've shown the other person you truly love him, you will feel his good will and love in return.

The problem is that we often want the result, feeling loved, before we actually do any real loving. Most of what we call love is based on some expectation of what we will receive. It is a love based on receiving rather than on giving. This is what is called love "for a reason." For example, if Rachel does a favor for Sarah, Sarah will feel some warmth and love toward Rachel and will want to reciprocate. That's a normal approach to love: While they respond to one another this way, it looks like a very great togetherness. However, as soon as the favor has been reciprocated, the love will cease, because it was based on a reason.

Similarly, if Reuven is attracted to Shimon because he is intelligent, he will try to become his friend. They may be friends for years. However, if someone else should come along who is even brighter, then Shimon will no longer be desired, and the friendship will cease. Unconsciously or not, the love was calculated. If you have something that appeals to me, my senses and my personality, if you have something I can receive from you, then I will love you. But as soon as that something disappears, my care for you will diminish. In Talmudic terms, this would be described as "once the cause has been abolished, the effect will be abolished."

With a little reflection, we will see that this kind of love was not really love *of the other person* at all. Reuven loved a certain quality in the person, similar, say, to the love he might feel for chocolate. He might say, "I *love* chocolate!" Is that love? Or is it not rather his wants and preferences that are of primary importance? The object of Reuven's desire, he whom he says he "loves," is just another delicious item for consumption. This is not love in the sense of putting energy out toward the other person; it is desire, which looks for the benefit "I" will get.

Often the benefit we are seeking in this desire we call "love" is really social approval. We "love" that quality in the other person that give us approval and sends positive feedback.

The primary reason people seek love and approval from outside is that they have little or no self-esteem. Too often, when two people meet each other, they are looking for approval and acceptance. This approach will almost certainly lead down the wrong path, for if love develops, it will be "for a reason"—I received acceptance, now I will reciprocate. But if the acceptance stops, the love will stop. It is important to realize that you are the way you are—not the way someone else wants you to be. "Take me as I am."

Only when neither is seeking outside approval can natural love develop between two people. This is more like love based on natural ties, like a parent for a child or one sister for another. This kind of love is called "not for a reason." Even though natural love is sometimes concealed in the course of family events, there is a hidden love which has no reason: the individuals love each other just because of who they are. They have a basic good will, and a desire to bring out the good in the other person — essentially, a desire to give of themselves. This is the kind of love that has no reason.

In any relationship, there will be some mutual attractions, some things you have in common. But that cannot be the main motivation for a decision to select a certain relationship. That would be love for a reason — wanting someone to share your interests so that you can receive positive affirmation of what you are doing in life. Instead, you must want to "feel the other person's soul," to appreciate and honor his or her uniqueness. Only then will you love for no reason, and go out toward the other person with good will and a desire to give of yourself. Then the commitment will last.

LESSONS:

» *1. True love can't be felt unless you think about others before yourself.*

» *2. Love and approval are natural, however Torah teaches us the hows, whys, whens and whats of implementing it.*

SAYINGS:

» *1. Who is mighty? One who makes his enemy his beloved.*

» *2. Love the person who criticizes you, and hate the one who praises you.*

» *3. Hillel the Sage said, "How does one love his neighbor as himself? By not doing to others what one doesn't want done to himself.*

READING:

The *mitzvah* of *Ahavas Yisrael* is well worth studying more deeply. See *Tanya*, Ch. 32.

Acting on the suggestion mentioned above — to view one's body with scorn and contempt, and finding joy in the joy of the soul alone — is a direct and easy way to attain the fulfillment of the commandment "Thou shalt love thy fellow as thyself," toward every soul of Israel, both great and small.

For, whereas one despises and loathes one's body, as for the soul and spirit, who can know their greatness and excellence in their root and source in the living God? Being, moreover, all of a kind and all having one Father — therefore, all Israelites are called real brothers by virtue of the source of their souls in the One G-d; only the bodies are separated. Hence in the case of those who give major consideration to their bodies while regarding their souls as of secondary importance, there can be no true love and brotherhood among them, but only [a love] which is dependent on a [transitory] thing.

This is what Hillel the Elder meant when he said in regard to the fulfillment of this commandment, "This is the whole Torah, while the rest is but commentary." For the basis and root of the entire Torah is to raise and exalt the soul high above the body, reaching unto the Source and Root of all the worlds, and also to bring down the blessed light of the *Ein Sof* [Almighty] upon the community of Israel, i.e, into the fountain-head of the souls of all Israel, to become "One into One." This is impossible if there is, God forbid, disunity among the souls, for the Holy One, Blessed Be He, does not dwell in an imperfect place, as we pray, "Bless us, O our Father, all of us together, with the light of Thy countenance," as has been explained at great length elsewhere.

As for the Talmudic statement to the effect that one who sees his friend sinning should hate him and should tell his teacher to hate him also, this applies to a companion in Torah and precepts, having already applied to him the injunction, "Thou shall repeatedly rebuke thy friend (*amisecha*)," meaning "He who is with thee in Torah and precepts," and who, nevertheless, has not repented of his sin, as stated in *Sefer Chareidim*.

But as for the person who is not one's colleague and is not on intimate terms with him, Hillel said, "Be of the disciples of Aaron, loving peace and pursuing peace, loving the creatures and drawing them near to the Torah." This means that even in the case of those who are removed from God's Torah and His service, and are therefore classified simply as "creatures," one must attract them with strong cords of love, perchance one might succeed in drawing them near to the Torah and Divine service. If one fails, one has not forfeited the merit of the precept of neighborly love.

Even with regard to those who are close to him, and whom he has rebuked, yet they had not repented of their sins, when he is enjoined to hate them, there still remains the duty to love them also, and both are right: hatred, because of the wickedness in them; and love on account of the aspect of the hidden good in them, which is the Divine spark in them, which animates their divine soul. He should also awaken pity in his heart [for the Divine soul], for she is held captive as it were, in the evil of the *sitra achra* that triumphs over her in wicked people. Compassion destroys hatred and awakens love, as is known from [the interpretations of] the text, "To [the house of] Jacob who redeemed Abraham."

(As for King David, peace unto him, who said, "I hate them with a consummate hatred," he was referring to [Jewish] heretics and atheists who have no portion in the God of Israel, as stated in the Talmud, Tractate *Shabbos*, beginning of ch. 16.)

9

Criticism

Friendships, marriages, and relationships have dissolved due to constant criticism. Yet we say that we value "constructive" criticism. What does this mean? How do we define what kind of criticism is healthy, and when? Sometimes we get upset with the individual who is giving the rebuke. Do we have the right to decide who may or may not reprimand us?

It is a Torah commandment to rebuke your fellow when you see him or her transgressing the Torah, the purpose being to prevent the other person from going astray. The Hebrew term for this rebuke is *mussar*. In Chapter 32 of the *Tanya*, the Alter Rebbe explains this commandment. Many people think it means that a person who knows Torah should harangue everyone else to get them to obey commandments. The Alter Rebbe says, on the contrary, the commandment only applies to a friend rebuking another friend. The Torah does not tell you to walk up to a person you don't know and "tell him off"; that would be absurd. The message the Torah is communicating to us is the importance of becoming a person's friend. Once you establish an ongoing relationship with an individual, you have made it possible for the person to want to hear your rebuke. Indeed, the individual will look forward to your advice and criticism.

There is a story of a young boy who studied Torah all night with a friend. Since they were awake so late, they were still sleeping the next morning when they normally would have been getting up to pray. The boy's grandfather walked into the room, woke him and said, "You're going to miss the morning *Shema*."* He continued to scold him for sleeping in, but the boy didn't respond. After the grandfather left the room, the boy's friend asked, "Why didn't you tell your Zaidie the truth: that you slept this morning because you were up all night learning Torah?" The boy answered, "When I listened to the rebuke from my grandfather, I was hearing sweet words. It isn't every day that I get to hear my Zaidie rebuke me, so I didn't say anything. I was hoping he might scold me more!" This is the way we should look forward to rebuke from a good friend.

I have been fortunate to have had a similar experience in my own life. For the last few years my wife's great-uncle, Reb Mendel Futerfas, has come from New York annually on a family visit. His primary reason for coming is to strengthen family ties. For me, however, it is an opportunity to receive constructive rebuke from an eighty-six-year-old Chassid who was put in prison by the Stalinist regime in Russia for more than nine years, one of the first "refuseniks." My great-uncle is a simple Jew, with no "shtick"! He rebukes me on matters having to do with my

---

* Jewish law requires the Shema to be said by a certain time during the morning.

character development. One could argue intellectually with some of his views; but I have realized that this is a unique opportunity to grow in a special way, so I take it all in. This is my only opportunity in a whole year to have such an encounter. For Reb Mendel represents the classic Chassid of 150 years ago. He recognizes that people are people, bound to make mistakes, but growth demands taking a good look at yourself. His rebuke is an expression of love.

Occasions do arise when one can and should take rebuke from a stranger. There is a Yiddish aphorism, "*Ah gast af ah vial zeht ah mial*": A guest for a short while can see a mile. Such a person can see what's really happening in your life. This may at first seem contradictory: What does a visitor really know about your relationships with your wife, friends, or community? Doesn't a person who lives with you daily know you better and really understand what's going on with you? The fact is that, although we cherish criticism from our friends, many times the people we know very well are blinded because they need favors from us, or some other factor prevents their being open and honest. However, guests as neutral parties can see clearly, and since they are leaving very soon, they have little hesitation in telling you the truth, whatever it is. Sometimes we will hear something from people who are relative strangers, but we should not dismiss it simply because they don't know us: They may tell us things that even our best friends cannot see.

Still, what if the person criticizing us has many faults of his own? That's really none of our business, since no one is perfect. As the saying goes, "if the shoe fits, wear it." It may be very true that the person giving rebuke needs rebuke himself, but that fact doesn't diminish our need to change. Our rabbis have advised us: Listen to what is being said, not to who is saying it. Accept the truth, whatever the source.

Growth depends on our recognizing the value of opening ourselves to someone who can give us constructive criticism. If we are unwilling to accept criticism, we will be stunted in our moral and spiritual growth.

While we should be open to learning from everyone, we must be very careful about taking on the role of rebuker ourselves. As indicated above, we first of all must be in a friendly relationship with the person. What do we do, then, if we see something about this person that seems to need correction, according to the Torah? How do we decide whether we are in a position to give criticism? The following are some basic criteria:

1. You, the person giving the rebuke, must not have an iota of prejudice against the other person.

2. It must make no difference to you, as far as your feelings toward him are concerned, whether or not the person listens to you. In other words, you won't be at all angry if he doesn't listen to a word you say.

3. You must be concerned for him, not yourself. If your concern involves your ego in any shape or form, then you have no business giving the criticism.

There is a letter from the previous Rebbe in which he bases these three points on several verses in the Torah.* In the Torah, the command to rebuke is preceded by another: "Do not hate your brother in your heart." The text following states, "Do not ascribe sin to him." The first means that there is a precondition to rebuking someone, namely, you must not have any feeling of hate toward him. If you have a previous feeling of animosity, then you must not rebuke him. "Do not ascribe sin to him" refers to

---

* *Letters of Rabbi Y.Y. Schneerson* Vol. 2, pp. 475-76

how our ego is involved after we give rebuke. If you feel your words are falling on deaf ears, don't say, "It's his fault, he's not listening." Rather, blame yourself: You weren't sincere in what you were saying. The words you spoke did not come from the your heart, so they did not enter his heart.*

The Rebbe gives a beautiful analogy to help us understand this thought. Before a doctor operates, he applies anesthesia because he does not want to cause the person pain. The same is crucial when we need to rebuke someone. Since it's a very painful process, we need to give anesthesia so to speak, meaning we must have a pure intent to heal the person, and not to cause him pain in any way at all. If this is our approach, we will surely be successful with our rebuke and, as mentioned earlier, people will be looking forward to having us rebuke them. They will perceive it as a sweet thing that's being done in their best interest.**

LESSONS:

> » 1. Look forward to receiving constructive criticism.
>
> » 2. To give rebuke you must possess three conditions: (a) no preconceived negative feelings, (b) no anger or frustration if the person doesn't listen to you, and (c) concern only for the other person, not for yourself.

---

* *HaYom Yom*, 26 Iyar, p. 57; see also 22 Elul, p. 89, and 24 Tishrei, p. 98a.

** See *Book of Discourses*, 1924, discourse beginning "*Im ruach hamoshel*," p. 218-219.

SAYINGS:

» 1. Ah gast af ah vial zeht ah mial: *A guest for a while sees a mile.*

» 2. *Cherish criticism, for it will place you on the heights.*

READING:

How and when to give criticism is discussed in the following translated excerpt of Rabbi Y. Y. Schneerson, *Im Ruach HaMoshel,* 1924, pp. 218-219.

Criticism: The criteria for giving rebuke

The Rebbe explains:

To understand the commandment, "Rebuke your friend," you must speak to the hearts of your listeners by saying, "How were you able to commit a sin or [alternatively] not do a positive commandment?" At the time of giving rebuke, he must also explain the punishment for the inappropriate behavior... However, the most important issue is that the person giving the criticism be humble. This means he should find within himself the same fault in some refined way...In addition to this humbling feeling, there needs to be remorse and regret felt by the rebuker regarding the very fact that such evil exists....

PART III:
SELF AND EGO

10

The Duality of Ego

Ego: we all have it! Is it healthy? The answer depends on how you define ego. Judaism sees ego in two different forms: (1) the arrogance we express in our day-to-day activities—a form of ego that is negative and intolerable, and (2) the inherent feeling that we exist for a purpose — a form of ego that is positive. Chassidus comes to teach us that even the second form of ego needs refinement.

There is an expression in *Tanya*, "*Yesh mispoel...v'yesh mispoel...*"* literally meaning, whether you are excited in this form or in another form. In this chapter of *Tanya*, the Alter Rebbe is explaining different levels of love toward G-d. He then includes this thought and states that, regardless of the level of love or the form it takes, it must be prefaced with *sur mira* — preventing

---

* Chapter 50, p. 263

yourself from doing evil—so that G-d can enter. The plain meaning is that before one can be inspired with loving G-d in a pure and true sense, one must not be committing acts contrary to G-d's will. Chassidus adds to the literal meaning the following adage: Regardless of your love or excitement about G-d, you remain a *yesh v'yesh* — an existing entity outside G-d. The saying is a play on the words "*yesh v'yesh*," putting forth the meaning that you always remain a *yesh*.* To better understand this adage, let us turn to a puzzling statement in the Talmud.

The Talmud records a statement of Rabbi Yochanan on the last day of his life. He said that he didn't know which path he would be taking, meaning whether he was going to Paradise for the righteous, or *Gehinnom*—Purgatory for the wicked, when he passed on. Yet, at first glance, this statement is extremely strange. Rabbi Yochanan was a great sage, a *Tzaddik*, a saint, a Torah scholar who never wasted a moment of his life in idle conversation; yet such a man asks where he will end up? It seems obvious he should merit the reward of Paradise.

One might argue that he spoke this way out of modesty. Indeed, Rabbi Yochanan was a very modest person; however, modesty doesn't preclude honesty. A truly modest person is honest in recognizing his or her own strengths; yet (s)he also knows those strengths are gifts from G-d. Such a person would not make exaggerated statements that seem totally absurd. Therefore, there must be a profound message hidden in his statement.

The Lubavitcher Rebbe explains it in the following manner.** On a conscious level, Rabbi Yochanan knew who he was;

---

* See *Tanya*, ch. 35.
** R. M. M. Schneerson, *Book of Sichos*, Vol. 16, p. 272.

however, he never took the time throughout his life to stop and analyze his deeper, unconscious self. To him, this would be a sheer waste of time in that it wouldn't contribute to his service of G-d. On the contrary; it would be the total opposite of what he was created for, namely to serve G-d constantly in a way that G-d's interest were the only reality, everything else being subjugated to G-d. For him to think about his own personal status—his spiritual fulfillment, his place on a ladder of perfection, whether there was buried in his subconscious some form of evil—would take time away from his mission of fulfilling G-d's will by doing good deeds. The pursuit of self-perfection at the expense of delaying to carry out G-d's commandments would be delaying the transformation of the world into a dwelling place for G-d. It would be tantamount to rebellion against G-d. He simply wouldn't do it. However, when the final day of his life arrived, and being a tzaddik, he knew his demise was upon him, he knew the Torah required a Jew to make an account of his entire life. This was not an expression of his ego, but rather his obligation as a Jew. Being honest, he had to admit that he was not really aware of the subconscious levels of his mind, and since there might be some subtle form of evil still within himself, he might not be tolerated in Paradise.

Rabbi Yochanan's selflessness, to the point of not wanting to spend time on his own unconscious, teaches us an important aspect of Chassidic thought. People generally think of themselves and G-d as existing simultaneously. The Baal Shem Tov, however, brought up a unique and illuminating perspective. He taught that it is impossible to have existing realities: It's either you or G-d. Therefore, "*yesh mispoel...v'yesh mispoel...*" means that as long as you sense personal pleasures, even if those pleasures be ecstasy from your meditation or other spiritual experience, ultimately, you still remain a *yesh*, which is the antithesis of G-d. The Talmud says regarding the arrogant person, "I [G-d] and he can't exist in the same room!" So too regarding the person who is still considered a *yesh*, despite his exalted spiritual experience, his self-awareness, albeit of the most subtle kind, constitutes a barrier between himself and G-d.

You may be thinking that this doesn't make sense. How can it be said that if a person feels his independent existence, this is negative? After all, didn't G-d give us our egos? And why would passion for G-d be negative? If a person were to be excited about mundane matters, then we could understand why that would be *yesh*. However, getting excited about G-dliness seems very positive. That is exactly the innovative point of Chassidus. Any feeling of one's independent being, one's separateness, excludes G-d, even if it is for only a very few seconds of time. At that moment, you and G-d are not united, and therefore it's a negative expression of the ego.

Practically speaking, we recognize that when we walk around feeling big and haughty, this is the form of ego that is dangerous for our character development. But there is another type of ego that is more refined, yet not healthy. Just as certain foods might not actually be dangerous, but an intelligent person would stay away from those foods, the same would be true for this second type of ego. The feeling that I exist and G-d exists includes that I have respect for G-d, and also that I acknowledge that everything I am and have is from G-d. However, this is unhealthy because we put ourselves on the same level as G-d with regard to "existing." As far as other matters are concerned, I agree that I am nothing and G-d is everything. However, from the perspective of being an independently-existing entity, we are both equal. This, Chassidus says, is paramount to a denial of G-d's existence;

because in reality there is nothing, in speech, thought or action, that exists besides G-d. "G-d is one" does not only mean that there is only G-d, but also that there is only one Existence. Only G-d exists, and all "other" forms of existence are merely an extension of G-d's existence.

It is only through recognizing this, and deeply connecting with this knowledge in our hearts, that we can really connect with G-d. Otherwise, we always will think of ourselves as having some sort of autonomy. The truth is, we don't: G-d ultimately carries out His Divine plan. This does not contradict the concept of free will, because G-d has given us the choice and encouragement to practice and participate in this plan; however, the plan is carried out with us or without us.*

What, then, is the true expression of ego from a Jewish, Chassidic perspective? It is the feeling that only G-d exists, and with His Divine wisdom and kindness, He has given me the privilege of participating in His plan. Therefore, when I see things happening around me that are contrary to G-d's will, I have an obligation to stand up for G-d, as his ambassador, and use my ego to correct the wrong. For this reason, we find many statements throughout the Torah expressed by great sages, that sound arrogant. Rabbi Shimon said, "The world needs me!" Maimonides claimed that by studying his code of law and the Five Books of Moses, we will have the whole Torah—that is, we won't need to learn any other commentaries. Similarly, Rabbi Schneur Zalman of Liadi wrote in his introduction to the *Tanya* that he recorded "all the answers to all the questions" concerning serving G-d. At first glance, such statements seem arrogant; but based on the previous explanation they are crystal clear. These scholars

---

* Ibid., Vol. 3, p. 976, note 19

had an obligation to let the world know how important their information was. As honest, loyal, and truthful salesmen working for "G-d's company," publicizing G-d's gift of Torah and mitzvos, it wasn't their own thoughts they were sharing; rather, they were sharing the knowledge of G-d as expressed in the Torah. The only difference between their works and the ordinary man's understanding of Torah was the fact that they were totally at one with G-d, whereas the ordinary man's character is distant from G-d. Our hearts and minds are not united with G-d in a totally selfless way, so for us to make such statements would be absolutely false and outrageous.

There is a story of a Chassidic rebbe who was accused of showing off. He told his accusers that he would announce publicly on Friday night in the synagogue that he is a nothing, and no one should come to him anymore. He did exactly that. The following Friday night, twice as many people attended the service. When the people heard him make the public announcement, they had immediately spread the word around the shtetl that they had such a humble rebbe, who publicly humiliates himself so as not to draw attention to himself and his greatness. This is the type of ego we should have.

This approach is also part of the Jewish educational system. When he was a boy, Reb Yosef Yitzchok was told by his father, Reb Sholom Ber, to address all his questions about Judaism to him and no one else. The reason was that his father wanted to raise him in a unique way, without any outside interference. His father instructed him to say the morning prayer known as *Modeh ani* by putting one hand on the other, and at the same time, bending his head slightly while reciting the prayer. (The reason for bending the head was to acknowledge G-d.) Little Yosef asked his father the reason for this. The father responded, "In truth, a

Jew should do whatever he is told, without asking why. However, since I told you to ask me all your questions, you may ask." The father called in his helper, Reb Yosef Mordechai, and asked him how he said *Modeh ani*. Reb Yosef Mordechai responded that he said it bent over, with one hand on the other. Reb Sholom Ber asked him why he did it that way. He said, "I don't know; that is the way my father taught me."

Reb Sholom Ber turned to his son Yosef and said, "You see, he does it because that's the way his father taught him, and his father did it that way because his father taught him, and so on all the way back to Moshe Rabbeinu, who did it that way. Moshe did it because that's the way Abraham did it, and Abraham was the first Jew to do it that way. You see, my son, none of them asked why, because you're supposed to do it without asking why."

Yosef was embarrassed and said to his father, "I'm still a little boy." His father responded, "All Jews are young, and when we grow up to be adults, we realize that we're young!"

The lesson is clear. What you think is the "obvious" adult approach—in this case, giving explanations—can be the exact opposite of what Jewish life is all about. This is very important when it comes to shaping the ego of a child. We must be careful to transmit the proper values of Judaism, including being a living example of doing as G-d tells us, without always asking why. This inculcates in the child the feeling that G-d is everything and that we are given the privilege to do His will. Moreover, as we teach this to our children, we learn it more deeply ourselves.

LESSONS:

» *1. Ego can be good and bad.*

» 2. He [G-d] is everything, and everything is He.
» 3. Think only about G-d; don't waste time thinking about yourself.

SAYINGS:

» 1. G-d says concerning the arrogant person: I can't live with him under one roof.
» 2. Stand up and be counted.

READING:

Reflect on the ideas of positive and negative ego while reading the following selection from J. I. Shochet, *The Mystical Tradition,* vol. 1, Chs. 7-9: "To Be One with the One."

Yichud and Perud

Yichud and *perud*, unity and division, can be said to be the pivotal concepts of Jewish mysticism.

Yichud is at the core of everything. All being, the whole of the creation, is as one body, the numerous members of which are fully interrelated and interdependent. However, just as in the analogy to the human body, the various organs and members are bound up one to the other, yet each of them retains its own unique character and quality. Problems for the whole, or for the part, arise where one's dual nature is ignored. When the individual shirks his universality, his membership in, and responsibility to, the others, the whole, and is preoccupied with himself, he commits an act of *perud*, division: mutilating the universe, "cutting down the shoots."

Perud, separation from the whole, in the mystic's view, is the cardinal sin, the very root of all sins. Separation is caused by self-assertion, egocentricity. It is tantamount to idolatry, creating dualism or pluralism. It is an infringement upon the ultimate *yichud*, the unity or oneness of the Absolute. For to take that stance is to establish oneself as a *yesh*, a "something," selfhood, a reality separate from, outside of, and next to, whatever other being there is. Thus it is a denial of the solitary unity of G-d.

The consequences of this tragic separation and division are not limited to the offending individual. The severance of a part from the whole implies not only the rejection of the whole by the part, but also the loss of the part to the whole. The whole body is rendered incomplete, deficient. It has become incapacitated with regards to the unique qualities and functions of that member. Hence the mystic's emphasis on *bitul hayesh*, the duty to negate, to efface, the ego qua ego, and the imperative dissolution in the whole; the concept of *deveikus*, to strive for the *unio mystica*.

Bitul Hayesh

Yeshus, selfhood or self-assertion, is the very antithesis of the principle of *yichud*. It is a denial of ultimate reality vested exclusively in G-d, who "fills the heaven and the earth" (Jeremiah 23:24); there is no place devoid of His presence; there is none beside Him.[*]

That is why pride and anger, arrogance and losing one's temper, as well as not caring about others, and so forth, are

---

[*] *Tikunei Zohar* 57 91b; see *Mystical Concepts in Chassidism*, p. 53, notes 16-17.

tantamount to idolatry.* For in all these cases man is concerned with himself, he assumes a reality for his ego.** In all these cases man has become self-centered as opposed to G-d centered, worshipping his ego instead of G-d alone. He may recognize the existence of G-d, even the supremacy of G-d, but also grants recognition to himself.*** He demands recognition for his honor, his desires, his absolute proprietorship over his possessions. At the very least this is dualism, which is no less crass idolatry than crude polytheism. This is the idolatry of which Scripture (Psalms 81:10) warns, "Let no strange god be within you."****

Of this self-centered person G-d says, "I and he cannot dwell together." That person is so full of himself that in him there remains no place for G-d. Of this the Baal Shem Tov taught: Self-aggrandizement is worse than sin. For of all defilements and sins it is written, "...Who dwells with them in the very midst of their impurity" (Leviticus 16:16); of the arrogant, however, it is said,# "I and he cannot both dwell in this world," as it is written, "I cannot tolerate he who has haughtiness and a proud heart" (Psalms 101:5).##

Bitul Hayesh thus means total self-negation. The ego, all and any forms of selfhood, must be nullified. It has no place in the consciousness of Divine Omnipresence.

---

* With reference to a) pride — see *Sotah* 4b; b) anger — see *Zohar* 1:27b; Rambam, *Hilchos De'os* 2:3; and c) not caring about others — see *Kesuvos* 68a.
** See *Tanya, Igeres Hakodesh*, sect. XXV.
*** See *Menachos* 110a; and *Tanya*, ch. 22.
**** *Shabbos* 105b
\# *Sotah* 5a
\#\# R. Ya'akov Yosef of Polnoy, *Tzafnas Pane'ach*, p. 76d (*Sefer Baal Shem Tov, Acharei*, par. 5)

The Duality of Ego

To be sure, there are times and places when there is a need to demonstrate pride. Honor is due to positions of leadership, and those holding such offices must safeguard that honor.* No less essential is pride in one's identity as a creature of G-d, pride in one's heritage and pride in being the recipient of G-d's Torah. But that is exclusively in the context of the service of G-d, as it written, "His heart was proud in the ways of G-d" (II Chronicles 17:6). It is never personalized. It is never in terms of self-aggrandizement.**

Bitul hayesh means conscious awareness of the ultimate nature of *adam* — man. The numerical equivalent of the term *adam* is 45, which in Hebrew consists of the two letters — *mem hey*, spelling *mah*.***

The Maggid of Mezritch notes that the word *adam* is a compound of the letter *aleph* and the *dam* (blood).**** The physical reality of man is essentially *dam* (blood; the vital principle of the body). The special, metaphysical reality of man is the Divine spark that gives him life, intelligence, humanity. This Divine spark, the *neshamah* (Divine soul) is the *aleph* — from *Alupho shel Olam*, the Master of the Universe.# To recognize the "Aleph — *Alupho shel Olam*" as our very essence is to establish our reality as *adam* in a consciousness that *per se* we are but *mah*.##

---

*   Cf. Kiddushin 32a-b
** See *Chovos Halevovos, Sha'ar Hakeni'ah*, ch. 6 and end of ch. 9; *Hilchos De'os* 2:3. *Tzava'as Harivash*, sect. 91; *Keser Shem Tov*, sect. 68 and 393; *Tanya, Igeres Hakodesh*, sect. XXV.
*** *Tikunei Zohar, Intr.:7b*
**** *Maggid D'vei Rav Leya'akov*, sect. 29; *Or Torah*, sect. 134.
\# Cf. *Osi'os deR. Akiva-I*, s.v. *aleph* (ed. Wertheimer, p. 348).
\#\# See also Zohar III: 48a that *adam* is the most sublime term by which man is referred to in Scripture; and cf R. Yosef Yitzchak (Reyatz) of Lubavitch, *Toras Hachassidus*, ch. VII; and *Likutei Sichos*, vol. IV, p. 1116, note 14.

To forget about the *Aleph*, thus employing self-assertion to the point of separating the *Aleph* from ourselves, reduces us to mere *dam*, mere plasma.

Individuality in Universality

It may appear paradoxical, but the emphasis on the universal, on the ultimate oneness of all, also emphasizes the particular. For everything created by G-d, thus everything that is part of the universal, is created for a distinct purpose, with a distinct task in relation to the whole. "All that the Holy One, Blessed Be He, created in His world, He created solely for His glory."[*] Every detail in the universe, therefore, is indispensable.

The toenails, no less than the heart and the brain, have their individual purpose: each one necessary to, and complementing, the others for the complete and perfect functioning of the body. Affectations of the toes become affectations of the brain, and vice versa. The ill health or pain of the one affect the well-being and functioning of the other.

To be sure, we do make quite clear distinctions between them. We speak of vital and non-vital, higher and lower, more and less important organs and limbs. We set up qualitative as well as quantitative scales of levels and values. Nonetheless, they are all intertwined, interdependent, interacting, with every particular adding its own contribution for which it was created. This contribution is its very function. To achieve it is to contribute to the well-being, the *yichud*, of the whole. To neglect it leads to *perud*, a division and defect in the whole.

In this context, too, it was said that everyone should always regard the whole world as being half meritorious and half guilty.

---

[*] *Avos* 6:11

The Duality of Ego

When committing a single sin, therefore, woe to him for turning the scale of guilt against himself and against the whole world. Thus it is said, "One sinner destroys much good" (Koheles 9:18), that is, on account of the sin of that individual, he and the whole world lose much good. On the other hand, if he performs one *mitzvah*, happy is he for turning the scale of merit in his favor and in favor of the whole world, thus bringing salvation and deliverance to them, as it is said, "The righteous man is the foundation of the world" (Proverbs 10:25).[*]

The significance of individuality is poignantly expressed in the words of R. Zusya of Annapol, when he said of his day of judgment that he did not fear the heavenly Judge's question as to why he had not attained the levels of the patriarchs, the prophets or even his masters; after all, who was he to compare to them? He did fear though, he said, the question of "Zusya, why were you not Zusya?"[**]

---

[*] *Kiddushin* 40b; Rambam, *Hilchos Teshuvah* 3:4. Note, though, that this weighing of the sin against virtues is not a simple mathematical calculation. There are a number of qualitative computations that come into play, and these are an exclusively Divine prerogative; see *Hilchos Teshuvah* 3:2; *Kad Hakemach*, s.v. *Rosh Hashanah*-I.

[**] This does not contradict the principle that everyone must strive to have his deeds achieve the level of the deeds of the patriarchs (*Eliyahu Rabba*, ch. 25); for just as the patriarchs did their best to live up to their obligations and potential, so can and must every individual.

11

Selfishness and Self-Esteem

We must understand a little more deeply the Chassidic concepts of selflessness and devotion to G-d. There is much to talk today about self-worth, self-esteem and self-development. Many self-help books and classes put a great deal of emphasis on these concepts, claiming that they are healthy and not selfish. They explain that a proper sense of self-esteem is the key to improving one's character. We have no argument for this. Yet it is important to see that the Chassidic approach, focusing on *selflessness*, goes much deeper, while automatically bolstering your self-esteem.

To understand this, we must first grasp two ideas which can be fundamental guiding principles. Reflect, first of all, on the realization that G-d created the world and all its creatures. It is only a short step to concluding that since G-d created the world, therefore I, the individual, owe Him the honor of respecting Him. The thoughts that go with this realization are significant, namely, I am something, and G-d is something. I have an obligation to subjugate my will to Him because, after all, He created me and is continuously giving me life. However, since He did create me for a purpose, therefore I am worth something. This thought is the source of self-worth and self-esteem.

The second fundamental idea following on what we learned in the previous chapter, is that all that exists in the world is G-d, and I'm a "nothing." This might seem to instill in a person a sense of worthlessness. However, looking deeper, we find just the opposite. Since G-d is everything and I'm nothing, yet I do exist, G-d must have wanted human beings to do something for Him. Since G-d continues to bring me into existence daily, I must indeed be important in His plan. I, the individual, am "everything" to G-d. As a result, I now have true self-worth and esteem because it is generated and sustained by G-d, the Ultimate Truth.

The second meditation has a far more profound impact on the person than the first. The first puts emphasis on the person, the second puts it on G-d. In the first meditation, the emphasis is on the person owing a "debt" to G-d. The result may be subtle, but is a subject of arrogance that has unfortunately been translated by many contemporary psychologists as self-esteem. In the second, a person's self-worth comes from a sense of purpose and direct connection with the Source of all creation.

A famous Chassid, Reb Yaakov Mordechai of Poltova, was known as an *oved* of G-d, that is, a servant of G-d. He used to daven many hours a day, and he mastered his bodily desires, never indulging himself. After thirty years of living this way, he became sick. The doctors told him that his body had become weak from sleeping on a hard bench. (In those days an ordinary bed was a mattress of straw, but even this was too self-indulgent for Reb Yaakov.) His weak body, they told him, meant that he could not expect to get well, and they gave him only a short time to live. Reb Yaakov Mordechai said to his friends, "My whole *avodah* (service) doesn't even equal one day of life in which I can get up and put on *tefillin* (phylacteries)." In other words, when he saw that the strictness with which he had lived had shortened his life, he realized that there had been something wrong with his motivation. Self-denying as he was, nevertheless he had been influenced by some minuscule amount of ego. His "egoism" would have been small and insignificant by most people's standards. However, had he done the straightforward acts G-d expected—to do the mitzvos, and to eat, drink, and sleep on a straw bed with the constant thought of being able to do mitzvos for G-d, he realized that he would have had another day of life to do such mitzvos as putting on tefillin, which have no ego at all because they are G-d's will. Put more simply, Reb Yaakov realized that at the "end" of the day — when no one else is around, and it's only you and G-d in one room — what counts is the pure act of donning the tefillin on your arm and head. This is much greater than practices such as sleeping on a hard bench for many years, inflicting pain on your body, which causes you to be sick and not be able to live that one more day to do just one more mitzvah!

The Torah teaches that one should work toward being totally selfless. If you succeed, you will truly feel good about yourself in the right way. On the other hand, if you go about correcting yourself by constantly thinking about yourself, the result finally will be a breakdown in your self-esteem.

This will explain a puzzling statement in the *Tanya*.* The

---

* *Tanya*, Part 1, Chapter 4

Rebbe says that the "garments" of the soul are greater than the soul itself! The term "garments" refers to the person's thought, speech and action in accordance with the Torah. The soul defines what is the make-up of a person, namely the individual's mind and character. The soul comes directly from G-d. But if so, the Rebbe's statement seems strange. The garments seem to be external. Good thoughts, words and actions beautify the soul, to be sure, as clothing beautifies the body of a person. But the person is not the clothing and is certainly greater than the clothing—clothes without a person would be worthless. So what could the Rebbe mean by saying the garments are greater than the soul?

The soul has a mission on earth, and therefore it is made according to the conditions of worldly life; it is made as an individual. Its requirements include physical and psychological survival of the individual. The primary instrument we have for individual survival is the ego. Therefore, while the soul is essentially pure, in its worldly manifestation it must connect with the ego in order to fulfill its mission. The soul becomes connected to "I" and all that the word generates, and it nourishes the desire for self-esteem. In this way, however, the soul acquires an association with selfishness—on a very subtle level, to be sure, but selfishness is there nonetheless.

The garments, on the other hand, are things that we do—thinking, talking and acting in accordance with Torah. Torah is the direct expression of G-d's will and wisdom. The *Zohar* says, "G-d, the Torah and Israel are one." When we do a *mitzvah*, we act out G-d's will directly, without any intervention of our own individuality. This is why the Rebbe says that the garments are greater than the soul itself. The garments are an objective expression of G-d, while our souls, as manifest in our earthly existence, are individuals with a distinct identity, and therefore not directly an objective expression of G-d.

Once there were two great Jews, one named Reb Isaac and the other Reb Yitzchak. Reb Yitzchak was in line waiting his turn to visit the Rebbe.* His old friend, Reb Isaac, passed by and noticed him. "Are you truly prepared spiritually to meet one-on-one with the Rebbe?" Reb Isaac asked. Reb Yitzchak thought about his friend's statement a moment and removed himself from the line. He spent the next several months refining himself — even though he was already a renowned Chassid. When Reb Isaac heard what had happened, he commented, "The longer Yitzchak stays away from the Rebbe, the finer a person he becomes. On the other hand, the longer I stay away from visiting the Rebbe, the coarser I become."

The point of the story is the power of self-improvement based on total nullification of the self. When Reb Isaac made his comment to Reb Yitzchak, Reb Yitzchak immediately realized that Reb Isaac's question was not an insult; it was meant to increase Yitzchak's ability to benefit from a visit to the Rebbe.

Reb Yitzchak realized that G-d is everything, and he is nothing without G-d. Without G-d, he won't gain from the Rebbe, because he's not a fit vessel to receive the Rebbe's blessing as long as he has too much ego. He wanted to be in the state of being where he had no self-worth independent of G-d's truth, as it would be expressed by the Rebbe. After he took the additional time to reflect on his relationship with G-d, he then went to visit the

---

* It is a Chassidic custom to have *yechidus*, a one-to-one meeting with the Rebbe. In this encounter the essence of the Chassid connects with that of the Rebbe, forming a union that goes beyond the normal day-to-day ways of relating. For more detail, see Posner, *Think Jewish*, Chapter 2: "Rebbe and Chassid," pp. 22-30.

Rebbe. He had managed to create within himself the feeling of total selflessness, and this was a key to his self-development.

LESSONS:

> *1. True self-help and self-improvement come when you're totally selfless.*
> *2. Self-esteem means the recognition of G-d as being all-encompassing.*

SAYINGS:

> *1. What's yours is yours, and what's mine is also yours.*
> *2. G-d says, "I and he (the egoist) can't dwell in the same room."*

READING:

Learn about Chassidic dancing as a means of gaining humility, which is one of the tools for selflessness, from the following selection from *Challenge*, published by Lubavitch Foundation, 1970, pp. 195-201.

The significance of Chassidic dancing

It has been said that the face mirrors the heart. Inner feelings

---

* See also *HaYom Yom*, 15 Iyar, p. 54: "The piece of bread that I have is yours just as it is mine."

are portrayed in facial expression. It is no coincidence that the Hebrew word for face — *ponim* — also means "inwardness." All feelings, like pleasure, joy, anger, surprise, disappointment and the like, have their own unmistakable facial expressions which are spontaneous and involuntary, and hard to repress or control.

Stronger emotions call forth additional manifestations; laughter, shouting, clapping the hands and so on. In the case of intense joy, even the feet are stimulated. People "dance for joy." Thus, dancing for joy is the highest manifestation of the most intense feeling of inner happiness, a feeling which permeates the entire body, from head to foot.

Chassidic dancing, that is to say, dancing as defined in Chassidic terminology and concept, is the outward manifestation of a most intense feeling of religious joy and ecstasy. Chassidic dancing is always done by males separately, as mixed (or social) dancing is prohibited by Jewish law.

Chassidic style dancing is not a new development. There are many references to dancing in the Tenach. Miriam the Prophetess danced and sang praises to G-d after the miraculous crossing of the Red Sea; King David whirled and skipped before the Ark of the Covenant. Most festivals, and particularly that of Sukkos, were accompanied by dancing from most ancient times. The Hebrew word for festival — *chag* — connotes circle dancing, and it is significant that the most joyous festival of all — *Sukkos* — was called simply, "the Chag."

There are two frequently-used terms in Hebrew for dancing: *mochol* and *rikkud*. The first means circle dance, the second — jumping or skipping. Chassidic dance includes both varieties, each having a significance of its own, as will be explained later.

The Chassidic circle dance is done in a closed circle, with one hand, or both, resting on the shoulders of the dancer in front. It usually, though not necessarily, moves counter-clockwise. There is no limitation as to the number of participants.

The up-and-down dance is more often done in crowded quarters, where there is no room for a massive circle dance. Individual Chassidim may perform a solo whirling or hopping dance, or it may be performed by two or more individuals. There is no set pattern of body movements in a solo or duet, though a duet usually involves "approach and retreat," and the locking and unlocking of arms.

The dancing is done to the rhythm or beat of a lively Chassidic tune or melody. Certain tunes and melodies are particularly popular on certain occasions and festivals. Both tunes (without words) and melodies (with words) are significant, not only in the rhythm and movements they call forth, but also in their variety of inspiration. Usually, an animated Chassidic tune without words will stimulate a higher plane of religious expression, since words are essentially limiting. (A person overcome by emotion is "speechless.") Some tunes may inspire teshuvah, others — a longing or yearning for the mystic union of the soul with its Source.

Chassidic dancing is usually accompanied by hand clapping from the bystanders, who join in the singing with gusto.

Chassidic dancing is practiced (at any rate by Lubavitch-Chabad Chassidim) on special occasions — Chassidic gatherings, or *farbrengens* (*hisvaadus* in Hebrew). These take place among Lubavitch Chassidim at the conclusion of the major festivals, and also on Purim; at the special Chassidic historic anniversaries (Kislev 19, Tammuz 12-13, etc.); at festive celebrations, such as weddings; on the arrival or departure of visiting Chassidic groups. Chassidim hardly ever dance during prayer, except during the Festival of Rejoicing (Shemini Atzeres and Simchas Torah, and Simchas Torah, particularly during *hakafos*, when dancing with the scrolls of the Torah).

In the vast literature of Chabad, which embraces every aspect of human conduct and deals with the esoteric as well as the exoteric, the significance of Chassidic dance also receives attention. Indeed, it is closely related to some very basic doctrines of Chassidus itself.

It would take us too far afield to discuss at length the various aspects of Chassidic dance in all their implications for the Chassid. Only salient points can be mentioned here, and they will at once strike a familiar note for anyone who knows Chassidic literature.

It is explained in Chabad that everything in the physical world has its counterpart in the spiritual realm.

In dancing the entire body moves. The whole body from head to foot is absorbed in the joy and exhilaration of the dance. However, it is the legs, of course, which play the principal part. The concept of "head" and "foot" is to be found not only in the physical body, but also in the soul. Moreover, this concept is found also in regard to the entire Jewish people, and in the Shechinah itself.

In the physical body the head is supreme, both in position and in quality, while the feet are the lowest part of the body. Yet there is a superiority in the feet over the head, in that the feet serve as a base for the whole body and carry it about from place to place. The head may decide where it wants to go, but it is the legs which must carry it to the desired destination. Without the power of locomotion which lies in the legs, the whole body, including the head, would be severely handicapped. Moreover, should the feet stumble even slightly, the whole body, including the head, could crash down and be seriously hurt.

The analogy, as applied to the soul, is that the soul also possesses a "head" and "feet." The "head" of the soul is that aspect of it which has to do with the intellectual qualities, while the "feet" are represented by that quality of the soul which is the source of simple faith. It is simple faith which is the basis of the Jew's entire spiritual life. This is true of every Jew, without exception. Hence, Chassidic dance emphasizes the great quality of simple faith which, like the feet of the body, can lift the whole body with the head.

As far as the Jewish people is concerned, it too constitutes a single organism. The Torah scholars, Rabbis and sages are the "heads" of the people; the ordinary Jew — the "legs." Obviously the legs cannot be separated from the head, nor the head from the rest of the body. There must be complete unity and harmony within the organism. So must there be complete unity and harmony among all Jews if the Jewish people is to be one healthy organism. Thus, Chassidic dance exemplifies this unity. For in the dance all Chassidim participate and are linked together, both those who are the "heads" and those who are the "feet."

As for the Shechinah — G-d's manifestation in the world — there is also "head" and "legs," as it were, termed in Chassidic literature *sovev* and *memaleh*. The former is the transcendental aspect of G-d; the latter is the immanent. Both are, of course, completely unified in the unity of G-d. The distinction is only valid in our human concept, not in reality. It is we who distinguish between the Divine attribute as manifest in nature and that which is over and above nature. In other words, there are aspects of Divine manifestation which we can comprehend in some degree, and those which are beyond the concept of either man or angel.

In professing the unity of G-d, as we Jews do daily and repeatedly, we have to understand, as far as this is possible, what this unity means, and in doing so, we cause the *Ein Sof* [Almighty] to irradiate our person, our soul, and the world about us. This is a profound and abstruse subject which is fully discussed in Chabad literature. But let it be said here that the unity of G-d is symbolically represented by the circle, which has no beginning or end, though we can speak of the "upper" part of the circle and the "lower" part of it.

The "mystic cycle" also recalls the famous saying of the founder of Chabad: "G-d converts the spiritual into the material, and the Jew converts the material into the spiritual." In other words, creation is a "descent" of the spiritual into the material, while Divine service, particularly the fulfillment of the mitzvos with material objects (*tzitzis* — wool; *Tefillin* — leather; *esrog* — fruit, etc.), constitutes the "elevation" of the material into the realm of the spiritual and holy. Jews complete this "cycle" in the scheme of creation, and make the unity of G-d a reality in our own experience. Here again, we have further significant meaning in the Chassidic circle dance.

The rhythm of the dance and the beat to which the dance is attuned, also have their particular significance in emphasizing the pulsating vitality that must animate Divine service.

The foregoing by no means exhausts all that can be said about the significance of Chassidic dance, at any rate to Chabad Chassidim. The inspirational quality of Chassidic dance has been greatly emphasized by the heads of Chabad since its inception. Though the occasions for Chassidic dance are few and far between in the course of the year, their inspirational effect is a lasting one, and their influence is felt in the daily life of the Chassid throughout the year.

12

Indulgence and Discipline

There is a Yiddish saying, "*Vos men tor nit tor men nit, un vos men meg darf men nit.*"* This means, what you're not allowed to do, you're not allowed to do, and what you are allowed to do, you don't have to do.

Although it may seem paradoxical or even contrary to common sense, this adage gives us the proper direction when it comes to the issues of permissiveness and worldly indulgence. Today, we look at our children and complain that they don't listen to us. We see our teenagers running away and ask ourselves, "Where did we go wrong?" We are indeed to blame, not for

---

* *HaYom Yom*, 25 Adar 2, 5703, p. 40; *Sichas*, 19 Kislev, 5745, pp. 871-873

something we said or didn't say, but for allowing ourselves to over-indulge in life's pleasures. We do this automatically, to the extent that we don't realize how fully we are consumed by the epidemic called "materialism." We try to calculate how much we should permit our children, while we, even if we are living quite ordinary lives, are inundated with television, radio and newspaper advertising that allows far too many materialistic ideas and promises into our lives—and begs us to invest our money and energy in more.

The only way we can know how much is too much for our children—and how little is too little—is by becoming living examples of self-discipline, not allowing ourselves to be programmed by the culture around us. Chassidus dedicates many pages to this topic, in order to teach that such behavior is not for angels in some other realm, but rather is part of everyday living.*

When G-d created the world He contracted His infinite light and created the world from His finite emanation. The infinite revelation was too awesome; it would have been overpowering for the universe to receive, so He went through a process of contraction, so that human life would be possible. This explanation sounds acceptable at first, but one could also ask, if G-d could do anything, why couldn't He have created the world so that, even though we are finite, we could experience His infinity so that we could benefit from awareness of G-d's full revelation, rather than experiencing only His finite manifestation?

One answer is that G-d wanted us to appreciate his creation, and the way for mortal humans to become involved and excited about something is by its being limited or restrained. When something we want is immediately given, handed to us on a "silver

---

* *Letters of Rabbi Menachem Mendel Schneerson,* Vol. 10, Letter 3313, p. 355

platter," we tend to lose interest in the object; it is no longer exciting. When, however, we have to struggle or make an effort to get something, we appreciate it more. As the Talmud says, a person would rather have a small amount that came through his own efforts than a great amount coming from someone else.

Since G-d wanted us to become intimately involved with Him, the most effective way to do it was by restraining His essence. In this situation, we are more likely to aspire to more and more of G-dliness, because we will always feel that we are lacking some part of G-d that is very important to us.

The attitude that "what is permissible isn't necessary," provides a level of restraint that gives us the ability to appreciate what we possess. By knowing and practicing this principle, we change our attitude toward materialism. Likewise, rather than constantly looking for loopholes to escape the rigorous details of Jewish law, we can see that G-d sent these disciplines in order to help us practice restraint: We can't have everything that looks, sounds, feels, or tastes good.

This does not mean asceticism or denial of our actual needs. Chassidus recognizes our humanness, but teaches us how to harness and elevate it. We can see this from the story of a woman named Chaya, who decided to consult her father-in-law, a great rabbi, regarding eating before praying in the morning. Chaya knew that by Jewish law it is forbidden to eat before you pray to G-d, and, being a pious woman, she did not want to disobey the law. But she wasn't feeling well, and her doctor had told her to eat something the first thing in the morning. When Chaya came to her father-in-law for advice, he said: It is better to eat for the sake of praying than pray for the sake of eating![*]

---

[*] *HaYom Yom*, 10 Shevat, p. 18

The lesson is that we need to be realistic with ourselves. If a person doesn't feel well and needs to eat to get into a better frame of mind to be able to pray, then it's the only way to pray properly. The alternative is silly: you will end up trying to pray, but what is really on your mind is how fast you can finish so that you can eat, and your stomach will feel better. From this we can see clearly the importance of eating and protecting one's health.

At the same time, there is a famous Chassidic tune with the words: "*Essen est zich, shlofen shloft zich, vos zol men ton, az es davent zich nisht un ez lehrnent zich nisht.*"* This means, when it comes to eating and sleeping, we do them naturally; when it comes to Torah learning and praying, it requires effort. It requires preparation on our part, and many times we are not eager to do it at first. We have to recognize that we are really slaves to our desires, even those as basic as eating and sleeping. But we can't say, "G-d made us this way, so we don't have to change!" G-d wants us to exert effort, to find within ourselves the infinite ability to overcome these basic instincts. The only way to do this is by thinking and implementing the adage, "What is forbidden is forbidden, and what is permissible is unnecessary."

To understand this more fully, let us return to that fundamental idea of the Baal Shem Tov, of which we spoke in earlier chapters. In Hebrew, it is called "*Ein od milvado*" (there is nothing besides Him), which means there is nothing else that exists, in any shape or form, other than G-d. The premise is the exclusion of any reality to anything besides G-d. The implication is that the world, as we see and perceive it, is one great expression of G-d's will and wisdom. We human beings are G-d's instruments to implement His will. When we experience ourselves as the

---

* *Sichas*, last day of Pesach, 1954

center of activity and forget who we are and what the purpose of the creation is, then we are inwardly affirming that there is something outside of G-d, namely "I." This affirmation of our ego would be the antithesis of G-d's complete and continuous union with man and the world, because it implies there is something in existence that doesn't belong to G-d. This teaching of the Baal Shem, that there is nothing outside of G-d, must be reinforced again and again, because we naturally think otherwise. But in reality, everything physical or spiritual is G-d's expression.

Based on this, we will understand a puzzling thought mentioned by Rabbi Schneur Zalman of Liadi, in Chapter 1 of the Tanya. He writes that the "animal soul" within human beings, the "soul" from which comes the basic life-force of our existence, is "*klipah*." This term literally means a "husk" or shell; in Chassidus it refers to the negative energy within the world, the cause of all bad character traits and harmful impulses. At first glance, the idea that this animal "soul" is the cause of evil makes sense, since it is easy to recognize that the animal part of us tends to want what is coarse and not G-dly. However, the first part of his statement says that our animal soul gives us the essence of our life-force. Why should that be *klipah*? It is our bare existence! If we say that it is the source of evil, it sounds as if we have no right even to exist.

If we return to the thought of the Baal Shem Tov, we can understand this. If we feel that we exist independently, that in itself is *klipah* (negativity); it is merely the husk or outer shell of reality, and to focus on the husk, without recognizing the reality within, expresses egotism. Even before we act, before we start utilizing our "animal energy" in ways that are outright harmful, the sensation of our existence outside of G-d is already not G-dly—it's already a mistake or a distortion.

An anecdote to bring home the point: Two Jews were sitting together and discussing whether a certain food product was kosher. One fellow said, "There is a rule in the Talmud that if you have a doubt concerning a certain item, look at its previous status, and base your determination on that. G-d created the world with everything in existence, and nothing was non-kosher. The Torah didn't come along till 2448 years later to outlaw certain things. Since everything was once kosher, when the laws of kosher and non-kosher weren't yet given, this can be said to be kosher now."

This fellow's opinion was that there could exist an item outside of the Torah framework and still be permissible, in other words, beings have a right to exist free from Torah. Hence, when the Torah explicitly states that a certain object is forbidden, it is forbidden, but when in doubt return to its original status—a part of a world exempt from a sense of purpose where things can be used any which way you will.

The other fellow replied, the world was created for a purpose, existence brings with it responsibility and obligation. We have a mission, a cause, we have meaning in life: to elevate all that we encounter to make the world a dwelling place for G-d's presence. Not everything can be directly elevated to G-d, some things must be discarded. The Torah is the Guide Book of life, informing us as to what we can elevate directly and what has to be rejected. Since the whole of existence is for a G-dly purpose, something which is not clearly useful in revealing G-dliness, has no "right" to exist—it must be forbidden. Man places no value on creation independent of G-d, mirroring G-d's view of reality. There is no true existence except for G-d's purposeful existence.

The difference between the two opinions is extreme. The first fellow is demonstrating an orientation in which he and the world represent an existence outside of G-d. The second person says that neither he nor the food has any ultimate reality: The only real thing is G-d. This sensibility helps a person not to indulge, even in things that are permissible. What feels good is not always good for you!

LESSONS:

» 1. *Not everything that feels and sounds good is necessarily good for you.*
» 2. *Restraint is the ultimate victory of freedom.*

SAYINGS:

» 1. *Vos men tor nit tor men nit, un vos men meg darf men nit*—"What is forbidden is forbidden, and what's permissible is unnecessary."
» 2. *Essen est zich, shlofen shloft zich, vos zol men ton, az es davent un lehrent zich nisht*—"When it comes to eating and sleeping, we do them automatically; when it comes to Torah learning and praying, it's not automatic.
» 3. *Better to eat for the sake of davening (praying) rather than to daven for the sake of eating.*

READING:

Study the following method of breaking your passion, from

HaYom Yom, 27 Shevat, p. 23.

My father writes in one of his *maamarim*: Early chassidim resolved in their souls to refrain from anything that is permissible (by Torah law), but for which they felt a desire and urge. This breaks the passion.

Part IV:
A LIVING SPIRITUALITY

13
Spiritual Perception

A student once told me, after one of my lectures, that he and a friend had virtually stopped having conversations on the phone. The reason was that every time they spoke, they engaged in gossip about other people. His friend told him this was *lashon hara* gossip, and that they had to stop talking on the phone, because even when they started talking about important matters, it always led to gossiping. I responded by saying that certainly gossip is inappropriate. But the way to deal with it was not to give up talking. Both of them should focus their conversation on spiritual matters. When their minds were involved and concerned about more sophisticated issues, automatically they wouldn't engage in *lashon hara*. Why not? Because they would be focusing on improving themselves, not on what they had to say about other people. He acknowledged that this sounded like a much healthier approach to life in general, and to gossip specifically.

There is a Yiddish expression, *Der kup darf liggen in hechera zachen*, which means literally: "One's mind should be engaged in loftier things." We ought to be mentally involved in spiritual and G-dly matters, rather than in day-to-day mundane and trivial issues. But at first glance, this would seem difficult: We must spend time on mundane affairs, we must think about them. Some of them are quite important.

Of course, many of our daily affairs *are* important. But when we look honestly at ourselves, we see that we tend to use our cognitive processes to deal with them in very mundane ways. Rather than integrating them into a spiritual perspective, we tend to follow the dictates of the mundane world. We lose ourselves to ordinary reality; it encompasses us and swallows us up, to the point where we actually think and believe that there is nothing else and no other way of seeing things. But there is more than one way of seeing even the most ordinary items in our reality.

An example: an artist can draw in two ways, either by copying another picture, or by having a vision of what he wants to draw. The second is the way of the truly talented artist. He begins with a geometric point, where he puts his pencil, and builds upon that. The result is beauty rather than a mere copy. The first artist might have skill and talent for drawing, but he has no vision. Why? He is occupied with what already exists, and the result is a mediocre picture that didn't contribute anything creative. By analogy, it is up to us to develop "vision," a kind of wisdom which will enable us to see the ordinary world from a spiritual perspective.

There was a rabbi named Reb Meir of Premishlan. In his community, the way to the *mikvah* (ritual bath) followed a path up a mountain, which in winter was full of ice and very slippery. Most people took a long, roundabout way, but not Reb Meir. He walked straight up the icy, slippery mountain. Remarkably, he always reached the *mikvah* safely without a fall. One winter, people from another city visited Reb Meir's synagogue and heard the story of his trips to the *mikvah*. They made light of it, saying it couldn't be true and that they'd follow Reb Meir and expose the whole thing as nothing but a fairy tale. When they began their trek up the mountain, however, they fell and hurt themselves. Afterwards, when they limped into town, they proclaimed Reb Meir as a miracle man. He responded that he was no miracle man and that it was really quite simple. He said in Yiddish, *Az men iz farbunden auben falt men nit unten*: "If you are connected above, you won't fall down!"*

The problem we have is the inability to lift our eyes from the "filth" and "shmutz" we are engaged in. We see a world full of problems, and we tend to see ourselves in the same light. In the Tanya, the Alter Rebbe discusses the inability of ordinary people to elevate evil thoughts.** If our focus in life is materialism and worldly matters, then regardless of how much we study, we will remain earthly human beings. What G-d wants of us is that we strive toward becoming "heavenly" creatures, in our human form within the physical world.*** The way this can be accomplished is by our being connected above—so automatically, we won't fall down!

A famous parable in a similar vein: A king had a son who was not following in his father the king's footsteps. The king decided to send him to a distant country, without any money or means of support. When he arrived, he needed basic living expenses. He saw that other people earned money by shepherding animals,

---

* *Sefer HaToldos Rashab*, pp. 53-55
** *Tanya*, Part 1, ch. 28
*** See *On the Essence of Chassidus*, ch. 1, note 6.

so he decided to become a shepherd. Soon after he began working in the fields, he realized how hot it was. He consulted his fellow shepherds, who told him they built little huts to protect themselves from the sun. "I don't know how to build a hut," he said; "I've been living in the palace of my father, the king, and everything was provided for me. I need help to make a hut." They replied that the king would be passing through the desert in a few days, and it was the royal custom that anyone who wrote a request on a piece of paper and threw it into his wagon would have that request immediately granted. The prince did as instructed: When the king passed by, he threw in his request for a hut. The king recognized his son's handwriting and realized he had ended up a shepherd in the desert. The king exclaimed, in great grief, "Look how far my son has fallen! If he would just ask to be reunited with me, he would have a hut, and no sun, and everything else that being with the king has to offer. But he can't get past thinking about his little hut! He has forgotten that he is a prince—royalty—*my* son, and now he thinks like a shepherd."

The moral is obvious. If we can't get past the mundane view of things, we will constantly encounter difficulties and hardships. We will try to invent bizarre solutions—like giving up using the telephone to cure *lashon hara*. We will end up living very uncomfortable, not to say boring, lives. If you build your life around G-d, if that is your beginning and your end, you will begin to recognize how life can be stimulating, and you can be creative, like the visionary artist. This is because your focus is on G-d, not on yourself. G-d created the physical world: He wants you to engage in phone conversations and paint pictures. Only elevate yourself, and your conversations and efforts will be elevated.

Even religious people can find themselves focusing on what could be called the mechanics of holiness, rather than taking a more elevated perspective.* An illustration: When Reb Sholom Ber was very young, his mother, Rebbetzin Rivka, asked her tailor to make a dress for her. She gave him the fabric. After completing the task, the tailor came to the Rebbetzin's home. Little Sholom Ber unwittingly put his hand into the tailor's pocket and found some of the leftover pieces of fabric. Having been caught in an apparent act of theft, the tailor turned red and ran out of the house.

Sholom Ber's mother scolded him for embarrassing a person. The little boy felt bad and decided to ask his father what was the proper thing to do in order to atone for embarrassing someone. His father, Reb Shmuel the Tzaddik, asked him, "Whom did you embarrass?" The boy responded, "It's bad enough that I embarrassed someone, I don't want to make it worse by saying who it is."**

The boy realized that another person had been hurt, and he did not want to hurt him further by lowering the man's reputation in his father's eyes. This was of utmost concern. The individuals involved could have become consumed by discussions of the exact details of who, what, and how: Exactly what were the circumstances and how bad was my sin compared to someone else's? But the childlike response, "I just don't want to hurt anyone," turns us in the right direction without ignoring the requirements of the law.

There is a story about a Chassid of Rabbi Levi Yitzchak of Berditchev, who owed money to an innkeeper. He had rented a

---

* This statement must not be taken to diminish the importance of following every detail of the Code of Jewish Law. Our discussion concerns the "approach," or attitude toward implementing the *halacha*.

** *Sefer HaToldos Rashab*, p. 8

room for a period of time, but times had become difficult, and he could not pay. His friends learned about his troubles just before Yom Kippur, and one of them decided to try to help. He went to ask for *tzedakah*—charity among the people of the town on *erev* Yom Kippur.

At one home, he found a large gathering of people around the table, sharing the festive meal that is customary for the day before the fast. Indeed, this group had become uncommonly festive; they were drunk. When he explained his mission to them, they said, "Sure, we'll give you a contribution, just share a drink of *mashkeh* (vodka) with us!"

The Chassid would never have thought of drinking just before Yom Kippur, but after a moment's thought, he decided that his Rebbe would probably approve, since it would help the mitzvah. He drank, and a man gave him money. He asked the next man, who decided to have some fun. "I'll contribute too," he said, "if you'll have another drink." He drank again, and went to the next person. The same thing happened.

A few drinks later, he had enough money, but he was completely drunk. He stumbled out the door toward his friend's house. When he got there, he gave him the money. His friend thanked him profusely. He replied, "It was nothing. Just get me to the shul for *Kol Nidrei*."

His friend dragged him to shul, where he promptly fell asleep, ignored and belittled by the other men. Suddenly, in the middle of the holy and solemn service, he woke up, jumped from the seat where he had been slumped, and shouted, "*Kum ata horaisa!*" This was the traditional call for everyone to get ready for the dancing with the Torah on Simchas Torah.

The men grabbed him and put him back in his seat. Some started grumbling about this drunkard they had to put up with on

Yom Kippur. At that, the Rebbe stopped his davening, right in the middle of the holy service. "You don't realize," he said, "what this man has done. He has spent *erev* Yom Kippur saving a fellow Jew from poverty and humiliation. As a result, he has leaped up all the rungs of the ladder in one bound—straight from Rosh Hashanah to Simchas Torah!"

This Chassid was connected on the deepest level to what G-d required of him. He was not distracted by mundane concerns, nor did he let the thoughts of others' disapproval disturb him. Yet we should be careful not to read this story as telling us that the "spirit" of the law—the love for another human being, is more important than the "letter"—the laws of Yom Kippur. In fact, the same Chassid who left his own home to go out and collect charity on another's behalf also insisted that he be taken to shul for *Kol Nidrei* no matter what. His attachment to spiritual concerns included doing G-d's will in every way, seeking the way to serve his fellows at the same time as he honored the holy day. This unity of spiritual perspective is our goal as well.

LESSONS:

» 1. *Connect to spirituality: Your corporeality will actually be diminished.*

» 2. *Pay attention to your thoughts and perceptions. Notice whether you are focusing on the material or the spiritual aspect of things.*

» 3. *Set aside time every day to study Chassidic teachings, which will elevate you to a different plane.*

SAYINGS:

» 1. "If you are connected above, you won't fall down!"
» 2. Der kup darf liggen in hechera zachen—one's mind should be involved in loftier things.

READING:

Reflect on how you can attain spirituality: *HaYom Yom*, 24 Cheshvan, p. 107.

In material matters one should always look at he whose situation is lower than one's own, and thank the good G-d for His kindness to him.

In spiritual matters one should always look at he who is higher than oneself, and plead with G-d to grant him the intelligence to learn from the other, and the ability and strength to rise higher.

14

Community: Farbrengen

Therapy is a big business in our society. People run from one therapist to the next, spending thousands of dollars and many hours of their time, often with little significant result. While this is a necessity for the healing of some individuals, there are many basically stable people who could derive greater benefit, in terms of personal insight and supportive community, from what I call "Chassidic group therapy." The Chassidic approach to self-improvement includes a unique and innovative event called the *"farbrengen"*— a Yiddish term meaning a gathering. At its best, it is a gathering in which Chassidim talk with each other about the private issues that lie within their hearts.

To understand the advantages of this alternative "therapy," we need to elaborate on the personal makeup of the Chassid. A few years ago, my wife's grandfather, Reb Zalman Serebraynski, passed on. After receiving the news, we were both shattered. While we were sitting down, absorbing the news, I said to my wife, "One of the lessons from your Zaidie's passing is the fact that the true Chassidim are slowly but surely passing on. We, the younger generation, are the Chassidim of the future. That is a frightening thought, because we know who we are, and we also know that we do not in any way, shape or form possess the quality of character that your Zaidie's generation had. We may do great things. However, who will our children look up to? A Jew who is basically driven by his or her whims, who is governed by the impulses of the heart?" Are we proper role models? What I realized is the great responsibility that lies on my wife and myself.

Who was this Chassid, and what made him so special? I had the privilege to spend time with Reb Zalman when I got married in Melbourne, Australia. Reb Zalman was a Jew who truly had accomplished making his mind govern his heart. Sometimes he was emotional, sometimes intellectual; but at all times he was in control. But he was not cold—far from it. He had a great love for his fellow Jew, and particularly for the students of the *yeshivah gedolah* — the school for older students. He looked after them as a father would look after his son, making them the focal point of his work, demanding from them cleanliness, Torah scholarship and *menschlichkeit*—humanity and integrity.

Reb Zalman taught *Tanya* until the last day of his life. He was energetic and able to adapt to any situation. Although he was a Chassid from Russia whose native language was Yiddish, he taught in English to all kinds of professionals. Moreover, he was courageous and committed. He had been an emissary of the previous Lubavitcher Rebbe. His task was to open yeshivahs in Communist Russia, where a person could face long imprisonment or death for teaching Judaism. Later, he was one of the pioneers to bring Judaism to the spiritually desolate territory of Australia — yet a territory which would turn out to be fertile soil for his teaching.

Personally, Reb Zalman always had a happy disposition. Some years ago, after his beloved wife Brocha had passed on, he wrote to my wife and myself about the need to serve G-d with joy—the importance of being joyful regardless of the situation. This was a true Chassid in the real world: He had made the teachings completely internal to his own life.

I was perpetually amazed at his ability to bring together two opposite worlds, that of the physical and that of the spiritual.

Did Reb Zalman need therapy when he had problems? I believe he did; but his therapeutic resources came from being with other Chassidim and studying Chassidus. In this way, he was able to delve into himself without getting depressed. Chassidus teaches how to deal with either spiritual or material problems in a direct way. It recommends getting together with others, because you will find among them people who are older and more experienced than you. When you share with them, you find answers to what is in your heart.

What happens at a *farbrengen*? Chassidic melodies are sung which have no words. They are called *nigunim*. Meditative and inspirational in nature, they often bring the singer and listener to the verge of tears, and many people have testified that hearing these melodies was the first step toward a true return to G-d. The wordlessness of the songs suggests the openness of the heart, going beyond the limitations of language.

Traditionally, some alcoholic drink is shared, for it is understood that a small amount of alcohol can be a "heart opener," for the mind often limits the expression of the heart.

We hold back our true emotions because our intellects build defenses, saying to us, "Everything is just fine the way it is; you don't need to change." When we toast "*L'chaim!*" we loosen ourselves from our corporeality and begin to open ourselves to the truth by sharing with others what's in our hearts and minds.

The leader usually tells stories of great *tzaddikim* of the past, or the heroic figures he has known in his own life. In the yeshivah where I attended many *farbrengens*, the stories came alive because one could see the character transformation that had happened in the person who told the story. Here was a living being who practiced what he preached, who had internalized what he had learned and expected the same of others.

After a few short stories, the leader encourages others to open up and, in simple English, "get into it." In response, people support each other in exploring their inner selves, acknowledging their difficulties, and struggling for inner truth. This way of opening oneself is healthy and thoroughly rooted in the Chassidic way of life. It is not just for Chassidim with long white beards who sit in yeshivah day and night, but for every Jew—even the younger generation—regardless of age, belief, or level of understanding and observance of Torah. We have to take advantage of such opportunities, because we now have the responsibility to carry on the teachings of our heritage.

During my years in yeshivah I had many opportunities to participate in these *farbrengens*. I use the word "participate" rather than "attend," to make a point. If we go to a therapist's office, do we listen to the therapist and then sit back and say to ourselves, "That's a wonderful idea—I'll consider it?" If we did, we would be wasting our money. If we want to change (and otherwise why would we be there?) we have to participate, speak up, open ourselves up to the therapist. The same is true for the "group therapy" of a *farbrengen*. To be available for change, a person must decide not to be a bystander, but rather a participant. Allow yourself to be swept away, touched and moved.

I recall some of the deep emotions I felt at these *farbrengens*. I wanted simply to let go of my ego and my pride, desiring only to be absorbed within G-d. For a short moment, the inspiration of the *nigun* was so powerful that there was no "I" who wanted to be one with G-d. There was only G-d, who wanted us to be involved in His Divine plan. I felt this connection physically, being together with other participants, like brothers without any jealousy or greed.

Sometimes the feelings aroused at a *farbrengen* can be startling. I remember a *farbrengen* with Reb Mendel Futerfas, my wife's great-uncle. Reb Mendel's message is that every person must be simple. Any form of ego or conceit has no place in Reb Mendel's world. He communicated this to me very sharply one Shabbos. My family was sharing a Shabbos meal with him when, as often happened, some of the yeshivah students from the neighborhood dropped by. Immediately, a *farbrengen* started, with enthusiastic singing. In the middle of the songs, Reb Mendel stopped and told the following story:

Once a Chassid came to visit the Rebbe. The Rebbe told him to fast for three days, then walk to shul and go up on the *bimah* (the raised platform used for the Torah reading). He was to say to all of the congregation that sending their children to the local Russian schools was forbidden, because the children were being indoctrinated with heresy. The Rebbe added that he should not speak to anyone after making this announcement.

There were many KGB informers in the shul, but the Chassid had no fear and did what his Rebbe instructed. Years later, Reb Mendel explained, he met this Chassid at the time when everyone was fleeing from Stalin. He related that, when the Chassid recited the prayer before retiring at night, unusual sounds would come from his nose. When he first heard this, Reb Mendel asked the Chassid if everything was all right. The man responded that, health-wise, everything was fine. However, the courageous act he had done years before in the synagogue, making the announcement in front of informers, had made him feel self-important. His ego had become inflated. Therefore, he was reflecting on this at night before going to sleep. The sounds were his expression of true regret, and a call to G-d to forgive him for the fact that there was a "bad odor" coming from his good deed.

Reb Mendel, as he finished the story, lifted his head, looking out from his overpowering eyebrows, and said, "Dalfin, did you get what we are saying?" This was an example of another dimension of "*farbrengen* therapy." I walked away thinking very seriously about my own ego in connection with my good deeds. And, even though he had made his point in public, I wasn't insulted because we were all equal participants. It was a tremendously cleansing experience.

You can probably find such a *farbrengen* in your community or one nearby, where you can become a regular participant. Adults and students are the usual participants. But parents should take their young children along too. My wife remembers sitting on her father's lap, listening to the older Chassidim recalling their days in Russia. She was only five years old when she heard one Chassid speak to another about a particular character trait but, she remembers, it left an indelible impression on her that remains even today.

A person must go to a *farbrengen* and become a participant in order to understand it. It does not take long to feel a part of the mood and to overcome one's initial embarrassment. You will begin to look forward to sharing with other Chassidim, for you will discover that they are the ones who truly care for you.

LESSONS:

> » 1. Study Chassidus.
> » 2. Participate in farbrengens.
> » 3. Discover Chassidic "group therapy" by going to farbrengens on a regular basis.*

SAYINGS:

> » 1. What a Chassidic farbrengen can accomplish, even the angel Michoel can't accomplish.
> » 2. Experience transcends—imagine yourself in a Chassidic farbrengen!
> » 3. The farbrengen formed the Chassid.

READING:

Reflect on the value of the *farbrengen* for bringing a different perspective to one's life, from *HaYom Yom*, 24 Tishrei, p. 98a.

A public *farbrengen* in general, and on Shabbos or *motzoei*

---

* Needless to say, there are times when conventional therapy is absolutely necessary; anyone with an acute mental disorder must seek professional help in addition to self-help and connection to G-d via Torah. Our discussion of the benefits of the *farbrengen* concerns the average person who is mentally stable, but seeking support and guidance through the difficulties of life.

Shabbos in particular, is one of the foundations in the ways of Chassidim and Chassidus. It is an opening and entry-way to the fundamental mitzvah of *ahavas Yisrael*.

At the great majority of *farbrengens*, the principle speakers demand of the participants that they improve their conduct and practices, designate times for the study of Chassidus and keep those times diligently, and that their study be directed to learning and fulfillment.

(The general concept and method of reproving another is well explained in the *maamar V'im ruach hamosheil* (*Kuntres* 30). Every chassid would do well to learn it thoroughly and take it deeply to heart.)

But this reproving at a *farbrengen* is only for such matters that will not cause any embarrassment whatsoever. This has been the way since the earliest days — one reproved another with love and deep affection.

15

Patience: The Nigun

Today's world offers us many methods to help us become more patient and accepting. People suggest meditation, changes of light, walking in the woods, being in water, going to therapy—the list goes on. Chassidic teachings and practices introduce us to a new and different approach, through the *nigun*.[*] Literally meaning a tune or melody, the *nigun*, in Chabad doctrine, is the pen of the soul, just as the tongue is the pen of the heart. We Jews have two "souls," two drives which enable us to function in the world. One is animalistic in nature, the other is G-dly.[**] The G-dly soul needs nourishment just as the body does. One kind of food for the soul is the *nigun*. In this way, the soul can raise itself above the constraints of the body and

---

[*] See Edward Hoffman, *The Way of Splendor: Jewish Mysticism and Modern Psychology*, pp. 160-66.
[**] *Tanya*, Chs. 1-2; N. Mindel, *Philosophy of Chabad*, Vol. 2, pp. 25-57

incorporate the body into the service of G-d. The true ability to have patience comes when you are able to learn and sing *nigunim*.

During my years at home, my father, Reb Aron Hillel Dalfin, taught my brothers, my sister and myself various *nigunim*. Usually, he taught them on Shabbos afternoons after we came home from shul. We ate, and then all of us children wanted to leave the table and run outside to play. He said to us, "Shabbos is a time to relax and sing *nigunim*, not to rush your meal." He made us stay at the table and listen to him sing. He would close his eyes and sing with tremendous devotion. After certain tunes he would express to us his true desire in life, which was to forget about all materialistic pursuits and cleave only to G-d. His feelings weren't saintly or angelic; he was simply expressing a Jew's true goal in life, namely communion with G-d. During the *nigun*, he went through a transformation, and we children experienced it too. None of us was superhuman; we were very simple, average people. It was the power of the *nigun* that made the difference in us.

Initially when my father would sing, I was bored. I wanted to leave, but he put his foot down and insisted, "You're staying here until I'm finished." I wasn't happy about that, but nevertheless I listened and listened. Years later, as a teenager in yeshivah, I developed a love for *nigunim*. I would fall asleep listening to them. It took many hours to learn each and every part of a *nigun*, but I had the desire and patience to listen to it over and over until I mastered the melody. Here was part of the transformation. Despite my childhood boredom, the impact of the *nigun* took hold and came back to me later in life.

Chassidim are known for their joy and fervor. Some people regard this as shallow and silly. After all, shouldn't man, the epitome of creation, be a serious thinker, a philosopher? How can such a person have time to sing and dance to G-d, when he should be occupied with higher things? Indeed, Chassidim are very serious and rational people. But there is something special in their joy.

A great rabbi once said that a person without a talent for *nigunim* doesn't have a talent for Chassidus! What could this mean? If a person studies, surely he can learn Chassidus. Why must he have a talent for *nigunim*?

Of course, this "talent for *nigunim*" does not mean a person has to be a talented musician. Rather, it means an appreciation for something special the *nigun* brings into one's life. *Nigunim* were created by great and saintly individuals who were expressing their yearning for G-d and their cleaving to G-d. The songs have the power to move others in that same direction. Thus a talent for *nigunim* is a movement in oneself toward G-d, a desire to cleave to G-d, ultimately to be lost in G-d.

Rabbi Y. Y. Schneerson explains the reason that a *nigun* has this potential. "The reason that singing can set up such a connection is that melody is made up of *movements*, and all movement gives rise to warmth, which is a vessel for vitality."* Movement creates energy and warmth. Just as a stone has no fire or warmth, but when you rub it against another stone, sparks will come forth; so a *nigun* with its *movements*. Musical movements are different sections within the melody, each generating different feelings and meaning. When we sing these *movements*, it stimulates our spiritual energy and results in a warmth which can connect us to the spiritual energy of those who

---

* *Likkutei Dibburim*, Vol. 3, p. 183. In the original Hebrew, the word for "movements" is *T'nuos*, תנועות.

created the *nigunim*, in their yearnings and movements toward G-d.[*]

Another feature of the *nigun* is that it is sung over and over. One may sing it many times; indeed, Chassidim often will sing the same *nigun* for hours. The purpose certainly is not to learn it well—this could be accomplished with a few repetitions. This is like the person who is so taken by a work of art that he gazes at it for hours.[**] This is not just a matter of admiring the talent of the artist in drawing, color or proportion, but of being drawn into it, becoming absorbed by it. If another person walks by and asks, "What are you looking at?" there is really no answer. There is no "you" who is looking. Likewise, singing the *nigun* enables one literally to lose oneself and become absorbed by G-d.

This is why a *nigun* is similar to Chassidus, and a person without an appreciation for *nigunim* can't appreciate Chassidus. The purpose of both is to become absorbed by G-d. With the *nigun*, knowing the melody is a step, but only one step on the path. Likewise, studying Chassidus is important—we must understand G-d, ourselves, and the universe through metaphor, parables, and morals from everyday life. But the purpose of the study is not merely to gain information. The novelty of Chassidus is to constantly strive to be absorbed in the unknown. Study is to be accompanied by contemplation and meditation on the thoughts that are connected with these teachings.[***] When the

---

[*] This might be an explanation of why some Jewish people sway back and forth during prayer services (known as "shuckling").

[**] Reb Dov Ber of Lubavitch, *Tract on Ecstasy*, printed in *Sefer Hamamorim Admur Emtzoie-Kuntreisim*, Kehot 1991, pp. 65-68

[***] Chabad meditation is all-inclusive, based on appropriate study of a text of Torah thoughts that deal with the creation and its purpose. The proper form of study includes reviewing the discourse at least four times. The student

student internalizes what he learns, when it is with him during prayer, then a different experience comes about. The material learned becomes an entryway into deep thought that activates other levels, and ultimately brings the person to a new level of experience. We can call this level "total transformation."

Most of our songs reflect only a shallow approach to oneself, G-d and the world, therefore they are sung quickly, without patience. So also many people go about their Torah study and the rest of their lives as well, in the same way. The result is emptiness and a rushed life style. However, when you develop appreciation for a *nigun* and for patience, you have sensitized yourself to be absorbed in the unknown and to have the truth about yourself be revealed to you, and you accept that truth willingly and joyfully. This takes a great amount of patience on your part.

The basic striving of a Jew is to be absorbed by G-d, the desire to be lost and absorbed in the higher power that is beyond our understanding; and this is what Chassidus helps us attain. Everyone should allow himself the time, energy and patience to be absorbed by *nigunim* and Chassidus; it's not just for scholars and sages, but for every Jew.

---

    internalizes the study, to the point that he remembers its content by heart, and can keep the thoughts in his mind during prayer. With daily study and practice over a period of time, contemplation deepens, and this automatically brings a change in the person's character. See Rabbi Sholom Ber of Lubavitch (trans. L. Danizger), *Tract on Prayer* (Kehot Publishing Society, 1993), and *Kuntres HaAvoda*. In order to understand Chabad meditation, it s obligatory to learn these two books with a Chassidic master. There are many other, non-Chabad, types of Jewish meditation. Many meditations, including meditation on mantras, are against Jewish law, and one is not permitted to use them.

LESSONS:

» 1. Nigunim *help you have patience.*

» 2. Nigunim *take you out of your mundane realm and place you in a domain of G-dliness.*

» 3. Nigunim *and* Chassidus *cause a person to constantly strive to be absorbed in the unknown of G-dliness.*

SAYINGS:

» 1. *Mit moach, nisht mit koach:* With your head, not with your strength.

» 2. Do not be hasty in spirit to be angry.[*]

» 3. A patient person has time for everything. If a minute is time, then that time is successful.[**]

» 4. The tongue is the pen of the heart; the song is the pen of the soul.

READING:

The power of the *nigun*: *HaYom Yom*, Sunday, 22 Tammuz:

My father said: A chassidic aphorism makes the head clear and the heart clear; a chassidic virtuous practice fills the home with light; a chassidic melody fortifies hope and trust, brings joyousness, and places the home and family in a state of "light."

---

[*] Koheles 7:9
[**] *Sichos*, 1940, p. 113

List Of Questions for Self-reflection:

1. Do I have real friends?
2. What are my priorities in life?
3. Do I consider myself to have a strong ego?
4. What kind of self-esteem do I possess?
5. How much time and money have I spent on therapists?
6. Define an emotional person.
7. Define an intellectual person.
8. Which of the above am I?
9. What is my perception of true love?
10. Am I self-centered?
11. What addictions do I have?
12. Are they chemical or emotional?
13. What are my good character traits?

14. What are my bad character traits?
15. How much time do I spend in thought?
16. Am I a religious person?
17. Am I a shallow or a deep person?
18. Do I accept criticism well?
19. Do I have self-confidence?
20. What are my cognitive distortions?

Index

A

ahavas Yisrael 86
anger 105
anxiety 44, 47, 79
Apter Rebbe 83
arrogance 97, 111
asceticism 123
Australia 140

B

Baal Shem Tov 66, 99, 124
binah 41
body 63
brain 22

C

C's (3) 41
Chabad 62
change 49-51, 53, 55, 57, 59
Chassidic dancing 116
Chassidim 61-62
Chassidus 21, 29
cheerfulness 44
chitzonius 24
chochmah 41
choose 73
cognitive distortions 16
common sense 72
community 139, 144
concentration 41
connectedness 61
conservative 26
control 24

criticism 89

D

da'as 41
deficiencies 39
dejection 46
delusion 30
depressed 42
descend 120
desires 25
discipline 121, 123, 125, 127, 129
Divine Spark 107

E

ego 97, 99, 101, 103, 105, 107, 109
ein od milvado 124
elevation 120
emotions 22 - 23
Ethics of the Fathers 77
exaggeration 30
expressing emotions 32 - 33, 35, 37

F

farbrengen 139, 141, 143, 145
fear 22
feelings 34
feet 119
flashiness 24
focus 41
free will 101
friends 76 - 77, 79
frustrated 42

Futefras Mendel 90, 143

G

garments of the soul 112
generosity 37
gossip 131
grief 22

H

happiness 40
hardships 40
head 118 - 119
heart 22, 24
heresy 143
Hilchos Melachim 45
Homlier, Isaac 24

I

immanent 119
impatient 26
individuality 109
intellect 27, 37

J

joy 39, 41 - 43, 45, 47
Judaism 71

K

kindliness 37
kiss 32, 34
kiss (chassidic) 33, 35
klipah 125

L

l'chaim 142
letter of law 137
Levi Yitzchak of Berditchev 135
loneliness 61, 63, 65, 67, 69
love 81 - 83, 85 - 87

M

Maggid of Mezritch 66
makkif 29
mashkeh 136
material matters 43
materialism 122
meditation 28, 150
melancholy 43, 47
melodies 117
mikvah 132-133
mind 24
Mindel, Nissan 41
Mindfulness 21, 23, 25, 27, 29, 31
Misels, Moshe 23
misnagdim 36
mission 99
modesty 98
music 36, 43
mussar 89

N

nigun 147, 149, 151

O

openness 62
oved 31, 111

P

Paltova, Yaacov Motel 32, 111
paradise 98
participate 142
passion 27
patience 25
perseverance 76 - 77, 79
pleasure 25, 36
pnimius 24
Posner. Zalman 36, 62
Premishlan, Meir 132
pride 105, 107
procrastinate 26
psychology 32
purgatory 98

R

rage 22
Rambam 45
reality 125
Rebbe 61 - 62
rebuke 89, 91
relationships 61, 71

S

Sacks, Jonathan 27
Schneerson, Menachem Mendel 12
Schneerson Yosef Yitzchak 32, 50, 51, 54, 62, 149
Schneur Zalman, Liadi 23, 125
self-development 115
self-discipline 122
self-esteem 85, 115
self-improvement 55

self-negation 106
self-reflection 153
selflessness 110
Serebraynski, Zalman 140
Sholom Ber (Rashab) 36, 52
simplicity 71
sincere 70
socializing 65
soldier 70
soul 63
spirit of the law 137
spiritually oriented 67
study 150
superficiality 70

T

Tanya 16, 140
tefillin (phylacteries) 112
Torah 33
transcendental 119
transcending the physical 64
transformation 151
truthfulness 70, 73
tunes 117
tzedakah (charity) 136
Tzemach Tzedek 22, 42
Tzernigov, Peretz 39

V

values 103

W

weaknesse 40
willpower 78

Z

Zohar 113

In Loving Memory

MEIR BEN YITZCHOK CHAZEN

28th of Tammuz 5751

July 10, 1991

In Loving Memory

BENJAMIN - BINYOMIN MASEF

21st of Iyar 5748

May 8, 1988

In Honor of

SHMUEL SHLOMO LEZAK'S BIRTH

16 Elul 5754

August 22, 1994

לע"נ האשה הצנועה

ויראת שמים

מרת **הינדא פריידא**

בת ר' אשר אנשיל הכהן

וויראסלאו

כ"ד שבט תשנ"ג

In Loving Memory

of our Dear and G-d fearing

Mother & Grandmother

HINDA FRAIDA

Bas Reb Asher Anshel Hacohen

Wiroslav

24th of Shevat 5753

February 15, 1993

The Dalfin Family